Pots and Windowboxes

MARTINA HOP

INTRODUCTION BY RICHARD ROSENFELD

 **REBO** PRODUCTIONS

To Ronald, with gratitude for his love and support.

© 1996 Zuid Boekproducties, Lisse
© 1997 Rebo Production Ltd.
text: Martina Hop
cover design and layout: Ton Wienbelt, The Hague
picture editing: Marieke Uiterwijk, TextCase
editing and production: TextCase, Groningen
typesetting: Hof&Land Typografie, Maarssen
translation: Evers Tekst- en Vertaalbureau, Bilthoven

ISBN 1 90109 440 5

Contents

	Introduction	5
CHAPTER 1	Container gardening	6
CHAPTER 2	The history of the container plant	17
CHAPTER 3	Containers of all kinds	24
CHAPTER 4	General care of container plants	36
CHAPTER 5	Plants for containers	65
CHAPTER 6	Plants and their attributes	128
CHAPTER 7	Glossary	131
	Index	135
	Photography credits and acknowledgements	142

Introduction

Pots are fantastic allies. They can extend the garden into even the trickiest areas, where there should not be a blade of grass. Areas like 'alleys', running from the lawn to the back of the house, and balconies where you don't get much sun.

One of the most outrageous gardens in central London belongs to an aging rock star. There's no lawn, just an enormous terrace packed with about 500 pots. Some are even hand painted. (You can easily do it yourself. For instance, for a striking blue and red striped pot, give it a lick of blue paint, and when it has dried attach five or six vertical strips of tape. Then paint over in red, allow the paint to dry, and finally remove the tape. Eye-catching, simple, effective.)

He's got rampant, climbing evergreens up poles creating punchy verticals – mainly ivies like 'Gracilis', and 'Melanie' which has frilled leaf margins with purple rims. He's also got wavy billowing bamboos like Fargesia nitida which has slightly purplish stems that easily grown 3m (10ft) high. And strong angular shapes with at least five different Cordylines, the best being the C. australis cultivars like Purpurea, and 'Torbay Dazzler'.

Most bizarre, he's also got a mock racing car built out of box topiary, with pale green plants for the wheels, and darker ones for the body, again all the plants in tubs. And I loved his topiarised tennis racket – again very easy to grow; take a central leader, and at about 45cm (18in) high, start training it to make the racket shape, then the handle. Later, you can add criss-cross lengths of string.

The plants were neatly selected so there were climbers taking over the walls, and shrubs on which they could rest. The strong rich red rose 'Parkdirector Riggers', which performs well all summer, and makes a backdrop for other plants. And the clematis … well at least 25 different kinds, with C. tangutica providing a rich late autumn show with yellow flowers and then silvery seed heads. There were even sweet peas climbing up cane wigwams, and six rich orange Japanese maples.

But if you don't have pots don't despair. Windowboxes are a marvellous asset. Two or three running in length should fill most of you needs. Basil fanatics can now grow at least six different kinds, including Mexican and Thai, besides the Italians, which are best for home made pesto.

You can even grow your very own garlic. Just buy the biggest juiciest bulb you can find, separate all the bulbils, and plant them vertically in the autumn. Water them in, and leave outside, no matter hard the frost, they benefit from a good chilling. Next spring, when the onion-like foliage turns yellow, fork them out, leave to dry, and eat. But beware. When you crush them before cooking (essential to release the flavours), the juice will spray your clothes.

For plant lovers there is an amazing palette. A bright lively recent favourite is the yellow Bidens ferulifolia, though you might prefer a blast of petunias, or even, with prying neighborurs, an impenetrable row of tallish Dahlias, not giants like 'Bishop of Llandaff', but Bambino Mixed which grows 45cm (18in) high. It should easily do the trick.

Richard Rosenfeld, East Sussex, 1997

Container Gardening

The great majority of plants will do well in a pot, which means you can always find a suitable container plant to brighten up a dull corner of the patio or fill in a space in the border.

Why are plants grown in pots?

In the past, the gardeners at stately homes and botanical gardens would grow plants from other parts of the world in pots and tubs because most of them were not hardy. They had to be brought inside in autumn to protect them from frost. Later, commercial growers also started to grow plants in small pots because it made them easy to handle. An added bonus is that container-grown plants can be sold to customers all year round, unlike plants grown in the open, which can only be dug up and sold in spring and autumn.

The Kumquat is a member of the Citrus family. This magnificent specimen graces the courtyard of Wijlre Castle in the Dutch province of Limburg.

Decorate a patio with container plants

As well as the commercial pot plants, which nowadays are all grown in black plastic pots, there are of course plants which are put in more attractive containers as an ornamental feature. Plants in decorative containers can dress up a patio and create a very special atmosphere. With some carefully-chosen tropical and subtropical plants, you could imagine yourself to be on a patio in some Mediterranean country - particularly if the sun is obliging enough to shine. With water plants in half-barrels, watertight pots or shallow containers, you can create a water paradise in a city garden. The manoeuvrability of container plants is a great advantage. They can easily be moved if you need more space on the patio for a party or want room to put more chairs out. And elsewhere in the garden, if there is an empty spot in the border where a plant has died back or finished flowering, the gap can be filled with a pot containing a plant in full bloom.

T I P

If you only have a few specimen plants, you can combine them with annuals and hardy perennials to produce a lush effect on the patio.

Plants for a pot or tub

Almost any plant can be grown in a container, provided that the type of compost used is right for the plant, and the plant is able to get enough water.

Acid-loving plants, for example, should never be planted in a compost with a high lime content because they will simply wither away and die, while plants that require a lot of moisture will obviously have to be watered regularly. Some plants -mainly trees- put down very deep roots, and are therefore likely to become pot-bound quite quickly.

All sorts of plants

The prime candidates for planting in containers have traditionally been annuals, or plants like pansies and pelargoniums which are treated as annuals. But perennials can also look marvellous in a pot or tub - hostas and ferns, for example, make wonderful container subjects. And shrubs like hydrangeas and *Buxus* (box) thrive in a container.

You can even grow small trees. You can also fill your containers with flowering bulbs and corms, such as grape hyacinths and begonias. And why not try making a miniature water garden in a half-barrel or watertight pot? A great many of the smaller water plants will flourish in these conditions.

Then there are the plants that have to grow in a container because their tropical or subtropical origins mean that they are too tender to

Miniature ponds made from half-barrels planted with selected water plants make a striking feature on a patio or terrace.

7

Oleanders are common in southern Europe, where they can grow into small trees.

survive our cold winters in the garden and will have to be brought indoors. If these type of frost-tender plants -herbaceous plants, shrubs or trees- were grown out in the border, they would be killed by the frost unless they were lifted with a great deal of effort, and probably damage to the plant too.

Simple is beautiful.

Specimen plants

There is no simple definition of a specimen plant. However, the term usually refers to a perennial plant, shrub or tree from tropical or subtropical regions. These plants are often extremely susceptible to frost and cannot survive our cold, wet northern winters without protection. They are planted in a container of some sort so that in autumn they can easily be brought into a frost-free greenhouse, conservatory or orangery to overwinter. They have to go outside again for the spring and summer.

Status symbol

In days gone by, specimen plants were grown primarily for their exotic fruit, or because of their culinary uses. The growing of spec-imen plants began with the import of different Citrus varieties. The juicy fruit, rich in vitamins, produced by these trees and shrubs were a welcome addition to the indigenous range. Later, they were joined by other fruit and vegetables, such as olives, passion fruit, sweet peppers, rosemary, ginger, and many more. Soon, however, the decorative value of plants from the tropics and subtropics became more

8

important. The great country estates all had to have beautiful gardens. A large, well laid-out formal garden was viewed as a status symbol, and an orangery with a large assortment of specimen plants in containers was certainly an indispensable feature. You can find out more about the history of container plants and orangeries in chapter 2.

The origins of container plants

A great many of the plants we use in containers come from the Mediterranean or areas with a similar climate, in other words hot, dry summers and cooler, wet winters. Many very popular container plants, such as oleander, rosemary and bay, come from Southern Europe. The Canary date palm is another native of Mediterranean regions. From South Africa we get the Cape plants. Most of the pelargoniums come from there, as do many of the plants grown from bulbs and corms, such as *Nerine* and *Agapanthus* (African lily).

A great many house plants, like the familiar *Ficus*, come from Asia, and so too do a number of specimen plants which people have been growing for a very long time. The citron *(Citrus medica)* was the first frost tender plant ever to be brought from subtropical regions to Europe. Other *Citrus* species also originate from Asia, as do the *Camellia*, *Hibiscus* and *Hedychium*. Central and South America have also given us a great many popular plants like *Agave*, *Datura*, *Fuchsia* and *Heliotropium* (heliotrope). And, finally, well-known

Here the container plants are displayed quite close to their winter quarters, which makes life a lot easier when it comes to moving them.

specimen plants like *Eucalyptus* and *Phormium* (New Zealand flax) come from Australia and New Zealand.

Something for everyone

Nowadays, specialist nurseries offer a huge range of specimen container plants, but most garden centres also have a reasonable selection. You can buy plants which could grow to tree size, but of course there are also plants that take up far less space than that.

Some container plants keep their leaves in winter, which means they have to be overwintered in a light place, others are deciduous and can make do with somewhere rather darker. All of them, however, must be overwintered in a cool but frost-free spot. There is something for everyone, and the fact that you only have a small garden or a balcony need not stop you buying one or more specimen container plants.

Annuals

The ubiquitous annuals like pelargoniums, lobelia, pansies and petunias are widely used in pots and tubs. These days, however, you can choose from such a huge variety of unusual annuals, which lend themselves to beautiful combined plantings, that it is well worth looking out for some of the less well-known ones. A good annual for pots is *Brachycome*, a smallish plant with very delicate leaves and a profusion of small, blue, daisy-like flowers (and there is now a new pink variety called 'Strawberry Mousse'). There are many varieties of

Bougainvillea is a frost-tender plant native to subtropical regions.

Nicotiana (ornamental tobacco) available in a range of colours and heights, and they will do very well in pots. Some of them have the added bonus of a wonderful fragrance. Other attractive annuals that lend themselves to containers include *Diascia* with their small, delicate pink flowers; *Dimorphotheca* with large daisy-like flowers that are white on top and blue underneath; *Nemesia*, with small, slightly trumpet-shaped flowers; *Nierembergia*, which flowers profusely and does not grow too tall; *Omphalodes*, with small white flowers; *Silene*, with delicate flowers in variegated shades of blue, and not forgetting *Verbena*, which is available in a great many colours and forms. Climbing annuals -which will trail attractively if they are not supported- include *Lathyrus* (sweet peas) and *Tropaeolum* (nasturtiums). The sweet pea cultivars come in a rainbow of pastels and soft, deep shades and they all have an intoxicating scent. *Tropaeolum majus* (the garden nasturtium or Indian cress) and *T. peregrinum* (Canary creeper) are both bright, cheerful plants which bloom all summer long.

Some of the plants sold as annuals can be kept from one year to the next if you treat them as you would tender perennials. They must be brought inside before the first night frosts and kept in a cool, frost-free spot over the winter. If you do this, there is every chance that you will be able to get renewed enjoyment from the plants next season. Plants

The charming flowers on this Brachycome *look like little daisies.*

The pendent tubular flowers of the Rhodochiton *are most unusual in shape and colour.*

in this category include *Pelargonium*, *Erigeron* (fleabane), with delicate daisy-like flowers in white and pale pink, *Pentas*, with clusters of tiny, star-shaped flowers, *Scaevola*, with striking blue, lobed flowers, and the climber *Rhodochiton* with its unusual pendent tubular flowers.

Petunias make ideal container plants and will bloom profusely throughout the summer.

Perennials, shrubs and trees

As I have already said, almost all plants can be grown in containers, although some do much better in the open ground. Really, this is a matter of trial and error - and if a plant does not thrive in a pot, it can always be planted out somewhere in the garden. The advantage of fully hardy plants in pots is that they can simply be left out all winter. These types of plants are the ideal solution if you do not have the space to bring frost-tender plants in for the winter.

There are many hardy plants that look really good in an attractive pot or tub. Perhaps the most attractive of these is the *Hosta* (plantain lily), which has particularly decorative foliage. Hostas flourish in shade, so they can be very useful in awkward corners. Other attractive perennials that thrive in pots include *Hedera* (ivy), which remains green and glossy all year round, *Helleborus* (Christmas rose, Lenten rose), with attractive flowers, fragrant *Lavandula* (lavender), Sedum (the house leek), many of the ferns and, of course, all sorts of herbs. Suitable shrubs include *Hydrangea*, with its imposing flower heads,

Buxus (box), an evergreen that can be clipped into any shape you like, heathers and *Euonymus*.

Trees are really only suitable for growing in containers if they are young when you plant them and are slow-growing, or if they are kept small by having their roots pruned, like bonsai trees.

Growers have developed an apple tree which is slow-growing, compact and slender, making it an ideal subject for a container - even on a balcony. Several varieties are available; they are sold as Ballerina or Minarette trees.

Bulbs and corms

The most popular bulbs and corms for pots are lilies and begonias. But there are many more plants in this category which do very well in containers.

Many of them come from tropical or subtropical regions and die back in the winter, which means they are easy to overwinter -pot and all- in a dark, frost-free shed. Examples include *Nerine*, with pretty white flowers, *Sprekelia*, which has showy red flowers, *Eucomis*, with unusual spikes of pineapple-like flowers, and *Oxalis*, which is available in a range of colours.

Watertight containers and barrels holding aquatic plants make an unusual and eye-catching feature. These miniature ponds can transform a patio or balcony.

Always look for plants which stay small and do not spread too much,

TIP

You can transform a balcony by planting a climber in a large container and training it along the railings. Pick something that is not too rampant, such as one of the large-flowered clematis species.

An attractive arrangement like this is worthy of a place on any patio or balcony.

Water plants

because you must be able to see the water. If your water gardens will have to stay outside in the winter, make sure that the plants you buy are hardy.

Provided you take a firm line with them, the pygmy water lilies, *Nymphaea* 'Pygmaea', will grow well in a half-barrel. Other suitable hardy water plants include *Caltha* (kingcup), with bright yellow flowers like buttercups in spring, *Menyanthes* (bog bean), with fringed, white flowers, *Sagittaria* (arrowhead), with striking, arrow-shaped leaves, and *Hydrocharis* (frogbit), with leaves like those of the water lily and small, white flowers.

You can use plants that are not hardy, provided that you can move the container to a frost-free spot for the winter. This group includes *Nelumbo* (sacred lotus), with strikingly beautiful flowers, *Eichhornia* (water hyacinth) and *Pistia* (water lettuce).

Nelumbo *(sacred lotus) is a tender water plant.*

You can achieve an infinite variety of effects with perennials in pots.

Preceding pages: Origanum rotundi-folium *shows to best advantage in a pot.*

The history of the container plant

People have been growing plants in containers for centuries. In the past, a collection of specimen plants was only for the very rich. Nowadays, everyone can afford several container plants in the garden or on the patio or balcony.

The first container plants in Europe

The earliest illustration of a plant being grown in a pot was found on the island of Malta. On the ornate altar in the Hagiar Kim temple, which dates from around 2000 BC, there is the image of an upright plant with dense foliage, growing in a container.

Pots to hold plants which graced gardens during the T'ang dynasty (AD seventh to tenth centuries) have been found in China. These pots were usually made from coloured clay, although porcelain was sometimes used.

In Europe, the growing of plants in containers began with the import of Citrus varieties. The first to arrive was the *Citrus medica*, or citron, which came from India to Persia in around 300 BC. The Romans, Hebrews and Greeks became familiar with this plant there and brought it with them to the west. The Romans started to cultivate the plants with their juicy fruit, and decorated their roof gardens with pots in which citrus trees grew. Later, they added other tender plants. In the northern outposts of the Roman Empire, they protected the plants against the cold by putting them in primitive greenhouses for the winter. These were usually constructed as a pit or trough covered with thin sheets of mica. Later, the very rich started to use glass to protect their plants. Amidst the ruins of Pompeii, devastated by the eruption of Mount Vesuvius in AD 79 and preserved under the hardened lava until it was excavated by archaeologists in the eighteenth century, there is a sort of hothouse with a glass wall and a

Terracotta containers are very much in vogue at present, but a coloured pot can brighten up a dull corner very effectively.

hot air heating system. Glasshouses like this were also used to grow other plants -roses, for instance- which could be brought into flower early. In the twelfth century the Crusaders brought the *Citrus* back to Western Europe with them, and the growing of plants in containers began.

The history of orangeries At first, specimen plants were only grown in botanical gardens. In order to protect the *Citrus* plants and, later, other tender perennials from the winter frosts, special little huts were built around them in the autumn and broken down again in the spring. These windowless structures were heated with open charcoal fires.

The first 'greenhouses' The first temporary structure of this kind was built in the Hortus Botanicus in Leiden, Netherlands, in 1594. But the failure rates with these little sheds were high. The lack of light and excessive temperature fluctuations caused most of the plants to succumb.

The introduction of glass In the seventeenth century, gardeners started to put glass walls on the south side of the huts, so the plants got enough light in the winter. These structures were not taken down again every spring. Instead, the plants were put into pots and tubs, so that they could easily be taken outside in the spring and brought back in again in the autumn. Initially these overwintering structures or orangeries, as they soon became known, were only built in botanical gardens.

Lantana *came to Europe at the end of the seventeenth century and soon became very popular with the owners of orangeries.*

The name 'orangery' reflects their primary use - the growing of citrus trees, particularly the bitter orange, *Citrus aurantium*. Later, orangeries were built elsewhere. But because glass was extremely expensive to manufacture and its use was subject to punitive taxation, only the very richest could afford them.

The largest orangery of this period dates from 1685 and was built at Versailles for Louis XIV. It is over 150 metres (490 feet) long, 13 metres (40 feet) wide and the same high, and has side wings each 115 metres (375 feet) long. In summer the plants in their containers were ranged along the terrace outside the building or deployed in the rigidly formal garden.

The earliest collection consisted solely of frost-tender or half-hardy plants from the Mediterranean, such as the citrus varieties, myrtle, bay and oleander.

Moving frost-tender plants

The plants that overwintered in the orangery were often grown in wooden tubs with metal handles, so that they were easily moved in autumn and spring. Ingenious hoists were designed for very big plants, such as trees and shrubs, so that the immensely heavy containers could be lifted on to special trolleys. Some of the smaller plants were sometimes grown in terracotta pots and urns, with special lugs. Using poles pushed through the lugs, two men could carry the pots into and out of the orangery without too much effort.

Nerine, a bulb that originally came from South Africa.

19

Widening the range of container plants

The discovery of the New World meant that more and more plants from tropical and subtropical regions found their way to colder northern climes. From the seventeenth century onwards, specialist plant hunters working for crowned heads and wealthy collectors were sent off to discover new types of fruit and vegetables and bring them back to Europe. Later on, plants were also brought back solely for their ornamental value. Transporting these plants collected in the wild presented a great many problems in the early years. Because they had to spend many months in dark boxes, most plants did not survive the voyage. In the nineteenth century, the English physician and botanist Nathaniel Ward invented a glazed box - the Wardian Case - which acted as a sort of mini-greenhouse, and the plants' chances of survival improved dramatically.

Many new flowering bulbs and corms, like *Nerine* and *Agapanthus*, came from southern Africa. The highly popular and ubiquitous *Pelargonium* is also a native of that part of the world. East Asia has given us the *Camellia* and *Citrus* sinensis, while the lemon, the citron, the bitter orange and the attractive *Hedychium gardnerianum* come from India. The popular *Fuchsia* and *Datura* (Brugmansia) originate from South America, as does the popular bulb *Hippeastrum*. From Australia and New Zealand came *Eucalyptus*, *Grevillea* and *Callistemon*.

Versailles still has a magnificent collection of specimen plants.

TIP

There are some magnificent old specimen plants in containers in the botanical gardens in Amsterdam and Leiden. These gardens are well worth a visit.

Ornamental value becomes increasingly important

In the nineteenth century the discovery of new glass-making methods and the abolition of the high tax on glass made it much cheaper to build an orangery. Cast iron was increasingly being used, making it easier to handle the panes of glass. Beautifully laid-out gardens with their associated orangeries became ever more important as a status symbol. In consequence the demand for new types of plants grew. These plants were chosen mainly for their ornamental value and much less because of their usefulness in the kitchen.

The care of container plants in the past

Real orangeries were empty in the summer, because the plants were outside on the terrace or elsewhere in the garden. But it became increasingly fashionable to build an additional wing or room on to the house where plants could live all year round. These extensions were called conservatories or winter gardens. Many of the plants grown in Victorian conservatories needed heat and high humidity, and coal fired boilers were used to provide these conditions. Hot water was pumped through the conservatory in cast iron pipes to achieve the right temperature, while the humidity was created by spraying regularly and placing containers of water here and there.

Following page. You can enjoy plants in containers all year round in a conservatory or winter garden.

A tub with handles can be moved relatively easily by two people.

Dormant period   At first, people believed that all plants from the tropics and subtropics needed an average temperature of about 21°C (70°F) all year round. However, it soon became evident that this temperature was too high for many plants: they became weak and susceptible to pests and diseases.

It appeared that these plants needed a dormant period in the winter with a much lower average temperature. Some of them actually proved to be hardy enough to stay outdoors all year round - some of the *Camellia* cultivars and the azaleas from Japan.

Many cultivars of the Hibiscus *have been developed, all with large, spectacular flowers.*

A number of Camellia *species are relatively hardy in Britain.*

Containers of all kind

When you want to put plants in pots, tubs or troughs, there are all sorts of containers to choose from - terracotta or plastic pots, wooden barrels and many more.

An old, weathered terracotta pot with a lion's head.

Terracotta pots In the seventeenth century people were using not only the familiar wooden tubs but also large terracotta pots to grow tender plants. Over the centuries these clay pots gradually gained in popularity, and the range of types and shapes consequently grew. In the days before the advent of plastic, commercial growers raised and sold pot plants in clay pots. These antique pots are very much sought after nowadays.

Pots from Southern Europe These days, a lot of terracotta pots come from Mediterranean countries like Italy, Greece, Portugal and Spain. As well as the familiar red terracotta, Portugal and Spain also produce what are known as blonde pots. These are a very light colour, and almost any plant will look good in them. Half-glazed pots are also very popular. In these pots, the inside and part of the outside are glazed, giving them a pleasantly informal look. These types of pots, which are machine-made in these countries, are on sale almost everywhere and are generally inexpensive. Hand-thrown pots are obviously more expensive, but on the other hand they are unique.

Oriental pots There are also a great many earthenware pots imported from the Far East. The large olive green pots with motifs like dragons or bamboo come from China. Because these pots are so attractive in their own right it is important to select the right plant to go in them. Plants that

bloom profusely or plants that trail over the edge are not as suitable for these pots as a single striking specimen.

From Indonesia and Malaysia we get the familiar, attractively glazed pots. If you want to use these pots outside on the patio, make sure that there are drainage holes in the bottom so that excess water can drain away. If necessary, you can drill a couple of holes in the bottom yourself.

Classic Versailles tubs with a simple ball on each corner, in quiet harmony with the standard bay trees.

Simplicity can be best

There is certainly a wide enough choice to enable anyone to dress up a patio or balcony and make it look really attractive. You can, of course, mix lots of different shapes and sorts of pots, but it can be extremely effective to choose a single type. By combining different sizes, you can create a stunning arrangement.

Several large, ordinary flower pots grouped together in the right place, or set out in a formal row, can also produce a very striking effect. The simplicity of the shapes allows the plants to be seen to best advantage.

Weathering pots

Terracotta pots can weather beautifully. Green algae and white lime efflorescence add to the charm and the natural look of these pots. If you want to accelerate the process in new pots, brush them with yoghurt or milk and leave them in a shady place for a while, and algae will soon develop. Some people, on the other hand, want to stop their pots from weathering and looking old. If you line the pot with plastic

TIP

Bulbous pots and ali baba jars are very attractive, but they make repotting plants a tricky business. You will either have to break the pot or damage the root system when you take the plant out. It therefore makes sense to grow annuals in pots this shape.

25

(leaving the bottom uncovered), the white efflorescence is less likely to occur. Algae are easily removed with a brush and clean water.

Disadvantages

Unfortunately, terracotta pots do have their drawbacks. To start with, they break easily. This means it is important to ensure that a plant in an earthenware pot does not become top-heavy - if it does, the pot can be knocked or blown over very easily.

You can prevent pots from being blown over, plant and all, by attaching three hooks to the rim of the pot and pushing them quite deep into the ground around the pot.

Prevent pots from drying out

Another disadvantage of terracotta pots is that a lot of water can evaporate through the porous wall of an unglazed earthenware pot - particularly if the pot is in full sun- so that it can dry out very rapidly. You can prevent this by lining the pot with a plastic bag or something similar. Make sure that the plastic cannot be seen at the top, since this would be most unattractive. Leave the bottom open (for example, cut the bottom out of a plastic bag) so that excess water can still escape through the drainage holes. You can also, of course, use a decorative terracotta pot as a cachepot and stand the plant in it in the plastic container it was grown in. If you want to disguise the plastic pot, you can grow a ground cover plant under the 'main' plant. This should trail over the edge and conceal the plastic inner pot. Make

TIP

A new earthenware pot will soon look old and weathered if you paint the pot with yoghurt or milk and leave it in a shady spot for a while.

*Facing page:
Old clay pots with a
few simple plants
can make a charming
feature.*

*This terracotta bowl
has aged beautifully
and is patterned with
algae.*

Simple earthenware pots in a bed of ivy.

An old wooden crate makes a cheap and cheerful planter.

sure that the plants you choose are compatible in terms of what they need.

Vulnerable to frost The last disadvantage of terracotta pots is that - unless you buy pots that are guaranteed frost-resistant - they cannot withstand frost. Water in the porous walls can freeze and expand, and this will cause the pot to flake or crack. Hardy perennials which could in fact be left out all winter will have to be brought inside anyway during frosty periods, if they are in non-hardy terracotta pots. You can protect pots left outside with a layer of straw or leaves, surrounded by plastic sheeting (bubble film is good), but you must make sure that the drainage holes at the bottom of the pot are not blocked. One way of doing this is to raise pots up on special terracotta feet so that the bottom is completely clear of the ground and any excess water can run away easily. You can buy these feet in a range of amusing shapes, including lions, frogs etc., as well as more straightforward versions. And finally, you can also protect your terracotta pots by burying them up to their rims in the soil. However, you will have to remember to water them in dry spells, because the plants' roots will not be able to grow towards the water as they would if they were planted in the open soil.

TIP

Because a new earthenware pot will take a lot of moisture out of the compost you put in it -and this will cause the plant to become dry very quickly- you should always soak new pots in a bucket of water for an hour before you plant them up.

Classic wooden containers The great country estates and palaces - notably Versailles - tended to use square wooden containers, which is why they are often described today as Versailles boxes or tubs. These containers were easy for the gardeners to make and repair themselves. This classic shape is still widely used in the gardens of stately homes and in botanical gardens. As a rule they are fairly simple, square boxes, decorated at most with a round knob on each corner. Simple containers like these are self-effacing and do not detract from the plants they contain. The tubs usually stand on small feet, which facilitates good drainage and also means that the lifts of a sack truck or similar trolley will fit underneath, making them much easier to move.

A moderately competent DIY enthusiast should not have much trouble making these square boxes. If you do decide to make your own wooden containers, you should use one of the hardwoods, which will not rot too quickly, or else preserve the tub against rot by painting or varnishing it, or treating it with an environmentally-friendly wood preservative that will not harm the plants. And remember to drill drainage holes in the bottom.

Round tubs Round tubs are very popular at the moment. They are often old wine or whisky barrels that have been sawn in half. The wood used in these containers has to be kept damp, otherwise the staves shrink and the hoops become loose, at which point the whole thing falls apart. If this

Old weathered pots have a beauty all their own.

TIP

You can prevent pots from blowing over by anchoring them with a few pins. Bend one end of the pins over the rim of the pot and push the other ends firmly into the soil around the pot.

happens, it takes a craftsman cooper to repair it. New barrels are often varnished or treated with some other preservative so that the wood cannot shrink.

Handles   Both square and round wooden containers often have handles which can be used to move them in the spring and autumn. Curved handles are extremely practical, because two poles can be pushed through them. Two people can then carry the tub without too much difficulty. Containers in which agaves are growing are particularly appropriate candidates for this method, since the plants' stiff leaves make it awkward to get close to the tub and the hard points of the leaves can cause quite a nasty injury.

Plastic pots   These days most plants, including specimen plants, are grown and sold in black plastic pots. These pots are relatively cheap and available in a wide range of sizes. The compost in these pots will remain moist for longer because evaporation only occurs from the surface. One disadvantage, however, is that these black pots can get very hot in the sun, and this can damage the roots of the plant. This is a particular problem with plants which press their roots against the wall of the pot. To prevent root damage, you can stand this type of pot inside another, more decorative container, or you can plunge it up to the rim in the border. Obviously the problem does not arise if the plant and pot are in a shady spot.

Left: Chinese pots are very attractive in their own right- the decorative value is accentuated by the simple lines of the ornamental grass.

Right: Many glazed pots come from Malaysia and Indonesia.

Other colours   White and terracotta-coloured plastic containers are also widely available, and dark green is becoming very popular too. White pots are perhaps too obtrusive and may distract attention from the plant. Terracotta-coloured and green containers, on the other hand, can be very attractive and, like the white ones, they require very little maintenance. They do not have to be taken inside in the winter, and the compost dries out much more slowly than it does in a real terracotta pot. Because they are quite inexpensive, it makes sense to use these types of containers in places where theft might be a problem - by the front door, for example, or under a window on the street side of the house. One drawback is that they do not weather attractively like real terracotta pots do.

Wicker baskets   Baskets have also become very popular in recent years. The natural material combines very well with most container plants. Wicker baskets are available in all shapes and sizes. Bright, exuberant plantings, for example, look very good in large, old-fashioned potato baskets. Use smaller baskets for an arrangement of annuals to brighten up the patio table. It is not a good idea to fill a wicker basket -even if it is plastic-lined- with compost and put perennial plants in it. The bottom of the basket will be kept wet for too long at a time and will eventually rot. It is better to use a basket for annuals, because they will only be in it for the summer. Once the plants and the compost have

Unless they are guaranteed frost-proof, terracotta pots planted up with hardy perennials will still have to be protected from frost in winter to prevent them from breaking.

A lovely combination: a pretty pink Verbena in a grey zinc wash-tub.

been taken out in the autumn, the basket can be dried thoroughly on all sides and put away in a dry place for the winter. It will then be ready in the spring to hold a new collection of annuals. If you want to display perennials in a basket, it is better to put the plants in a plastic or clay pot, and stand this in the basket. Then, if the basket gets too wet, you can always take the inner pot out for a while and leave the basket upside down in the sun to dry.

A miniature rock garden has been created in this old sink, using alpines and small conifers.

Concrete containers

Concrete planters can also be very decorative, but this depends very much on how they are planted up. Because concrete containers are often very large and rough, the plants need to be quite bold and striking too. Small, delicate plants will not look at home in a concrete trough. Old stone sinks are often planted up as miniature rock gardens, and this can be very effective if the plants are kept in proportion - with one another, but more importantly with the container. For instance, when you are creating a miniature rock garden like this, always make sure that you give it some height by including a bonsai tree or an upright shrub, otherwise the whole thing will be too flat and not in proportion with the large, shallow sink.

Facing page: By letting the bottom of a wicker basket dry out thoroughly from time to time you will prevent it from going mouldy and rotting.

Frost-resistant containers

You can sometimes find frost-resistant concrete containers, and because they are generally on the heavy side, it is a great advantage not to have to move them. However, these pots and troughs are rather pricy.

Making your own concrete container

You can make a 'concrete' container yourself. Start with two cardboard boxes, one of which fits inside the other leaving a gap of about 3 to 5 cm (1 to 2 inches) all round. Wrap a piece of fine-meshed chicken wire around the outside of the smaller box. Mix together equal parts of cement, coarse sand and peat, and add enough water to produce a stiffish mixture. Put a layer of about 3 to 5 cm (1 to 2 inches) thick in the bottom of the larger box. Use a few short lengths of PVC tubing to make some drainage holes in the cement base. Then put the smaller box on the cement base, taking care that the space is the same all round.

Fill this space with the cement mix. Stir gently with a stick to eliminate large air pockets. If necessary, you can reinforce the outer box with a wooden framework or strong tape. You will have to wait six to eight weeks for the mixture to harden completely before you remove the cardboard boxes.

The chicken wire stays in the cement. You can use a steel brush to smooth down any unsightly sharp edges. If you find that there are holes in the outer wall, you can plug them with a rock plant, such as an alpine or a small fern. As far as planting up the rest of the container is concerned - I leave it to your imagination!

Old wine casks, one left intact and the other sawn in half, provide the water feature in this garden.

Other containers

As well as the traditional pots and tubs we have already looked at, there are of course lots of other, possibly less obvious containers you can use as planters. Antique urns are very attractive, but also very expensive. They can be rather grand, so you need to be sure that they are in keeping with the patio or the rest of the garden. Wire hanging baskets, cast iron and lead containers etc. are all very good for brightening up a dull corner. And then there are all sorts of containers that did not start life as planters - old zinc or enamel pails, kettles, watering cans, paint cans, drinking fountains and so forth.

It is more elegant to plant up just one unusual object and place it in a prominent position, than to crowd a lot of different containers together. If you use a lot of unrelated containers in the same place, it can be very untidy looking and the effect you are aiming for can be ruined. In any event make sure that the planting blends well with the container. Some plants look much better in a simple pot than in a very ornate container.

And always remember that every container must have a drainage hole in the bottom to prevent the roots of the plants from rotting.

The more irregular the shape of a concrete container, the better.

A selection of annuals in a wicker basket- pick them up and put them anywhere.

General care of container plants

If plants are to flourish in pots, they

do need to be looked after.

Most plants are fairly easy to care for,

but some need special attention.

Natural habitat   A number of factors govern whether or not a plant will grow in a particular place. The most important are the type of soil, the amount of light, the availability of water and the ambient temperature. A plant may well have adapted itself to extreme circumstances -very poor soil, for instance- but this does not mean to say that it cannot grow in spots where more nutrients are available to it. In the wild, however, competition from other plants will be much greater in a richer soil, so that some plants get little if any chance to establish themselves there. In places where there is no competition, such as in a pot or tub on your patio, there is really no need to grow plants in the same conditions, in this case in poor soil. Low temperatures are a factor that limits the plants you can grow. Frost-tender plants cannot withstand the frosts that occur in the temperate regions and have to be given protection against them. A lack of light and a shortage of water will also be fatal to plants that have not adapted to these sorts of conditions.

A hydrangea needs a lot of water. Provided you keep the compost moist at all times it will flower for a very long time.

Learning by trial and error   When specimen plants were first brought to Europe, it was generally assumed that the plants from the tropics needed a high temperature all year round. During cold periods they were kept in heated greenhouses or warm rooms, but the majority of these plants soon fell prey to all sorts of insect pests, moulds and diseases. The plants which did thrive in these warm conditions later became very popular

as house plants, but the rest obviously needed different treatment. The regular airing of the greenhouses brought about some improvement, but it was not the real answer. It soon became clear that a great many plants, even those indigenous to the tropics, needed a period of dormancy with lower temperatures during the winter. Some plants dropped their leaves when the temperature dropped, so that it was possible to overwinter them in a dark place. This left valuable greenhouse space for evergreen types.

In the early days there was a lot of confusion about the composition of the growing medium.

Importing special soil from the plant's country of origin was obviously a prohibitively expensive exercise, so gardeners started to experiment with their own mixtures of leaf mould, sharp sand, garden soil and well-rotted farmyard manure. Clay or peat was sometimes added to the blend, but if these materials were not available in the vicinity they were simply omitted. Most plants seemed to thrive on these specially developed mixes.

Thanks to the efforts of gardeners down the centuries, experimenting with composts, summer and winter temperatures, positions in sun or shade and so on, we now have a very accurate idea of the conditions that best suit different types of plants. But our own experience is still

Foliage plants like box *and* laurel *need relatively high levels of nitrogen for healthy growth.*

The Fuchsia *needs a period of rest in the winter to flower well the following summer.*

very important, and our own experiments can sometimes produce results that are just as good -if not better- than those we get from going by the book.

The olive, Olea, *prefers chalky soil.*

Compost and nutrients

The best time to repot a plant is in the spring, when it is just starting back into growth and needs a lot of nutrients. Fresh potting compost contains lots of nutrients from which the plant can derive maximum benefit.

The true container plant enthusiast will make his own planting mixture, tailoring it to the needs of specific plants. But all garden centres nowadays sell general purpose potting composts which do the job very well.

General purpose potting compost

General purpose potting compost usually consists of six parts topsoil, two parts peat and one part sand. Lime is often added to make the compost less acid, together with inorganic fertilizers to improve fertility. The sand keeps the compost light so that there is enough oxygen in it for the roots and excess water can drain away quickly. The soil makes the compost very rich in humus, so that it can absorb a lot of water which is gradually released to the plants. However, if you let a compost which contains a lot of peat dry right out you will find it almost impossible to re-wet it, so it is important to make sure that this type of compost is kept moist. You can add extra ingredients to general purpose potting compost for plants with special requirements. For plants that like an alkaline soil, such as *Olea* (olive), you can add lime. For lime-haters like camellias and myrtles, you must use a compost without any lime in it. Ericaceous plants (heathers, etc.) must have an acid soil. For these plants you can add some extra peat to general purpose compost. Special ericaceous composts are also readily available at garden centres. Many container plants, particularly the older ones, benefit from the addition of a little clay or loam. You should be able to get this at the garden centre.

In areas with a clay soil, you can add the soil from molehills to ordinary compost. The structure of the soil in molehills is beautifully light. If you dig soil out of a garden or field, it is advisable to break it up very thoroughly to create a fine tilth, or leave it to freeze so that it breaks up. Gross feeders like *Datura* and *Cestrum* will thank you for a handful of well-rotted farmyard manure in the compost.

The properties of different soil types

I should like to run through the properties of the different soil types and nutrients here so that you will be able to work out for yourself what will suit particular plants.

The house leek needs little in the way of water and nutrients.

from a deficiency of these trace elements. In this case, however, the discolouration starts in the young leaves at the tip of a shoot. Other important trace elements are iodine, arsenic, boron, zinc, copper, fluorine, cobalt and molybdenum. These are generally present in sufficient quantities in ordinary potting compost and in general purpose fertilizers.

The Pelargonium *(geranium) does not like getting its feet wet so make sure the drainage is good.*

General purpose fertilizers

Most general purpose fertilizers consist of nitrogen (N), phosphate (P) and potash (K) in different proportions and a small percentage of trace elements. Three figures on the packet indicate the proportions of N, P and K. There are special types of fertilizer available for particular types of plant. You can get special fertilizers for ericaceous plants (7+7+17), for conifers (5+5+20), for pelargoniums (5+6+7), for foliage plants (15+5+10) and so on. The nutrients in these fertilizers are specifically tailored to the needs of the plants concerned.

These fast-acting feeds should only be used during the growing season, usually once a week or once every other week depending on the plant's needs. Do not be tempted to use more than the amount stated on the packet. In high concentrations, these feeds can cause scorching and will do the plant more harm than good. If in doubt, make the solution more dilute rather than too strong. Plants that have just been repotted or have come direct from the grower will not need any additional feeding in the first six weeks. Cuttings and young

Pages 42-43: Check plants for pests and diseases regularly - particularly if you have a whole collection grouped together. Rapid action can prevent a disaster.

plants likewise do not need much extra fertilizer. You should not feed any plants at all after the end of August. This gives them the chance to start getting ready for their dormant period in the winter. Plants which carry on growing in a warm place throughout the winter do need some feeding during the winter, but they will generally not want as much as they do in the summer.

Whitefly can be a problem with Hibiscus.

Watering   Plants in containers are wholly dependent on their owner for water. After all, they cannot send their roots down looking for water at a deeper level as plants growing in the open ground can do.

Zomer   During hot, dry periods you will have to water container plants every day - and some species will actually need watering twice a day. You should never use cold water. Let the water warm up slightly in the sun (to about 18°C [64°F]) or add some hot water to it. Some plants, like *Nerium oleander*, prefer the water to be even warmer than this (20-25°C [68-77°F]). Plants in a shady spot will need less water than plants in full sun. Plants in terracotta pots need more water than plants in a wooden barrel or plastic pot, because a significant amount of water evaporates through the porous walls. You can prevent excessive evaporation by lining a terracotta pot with plastic (being sure to leave the bottom free). You can feel whether a plant needs water or not by poking your finger into the soil and

45

Hibiscus huegelei
'Trumpet Serenade'
can be overwintered
in the house.
You will have to
water and mist it
regularly.

judging the moisture of the soil under the top layer. If a plant's leaves start to droop this can also be a sign that it needs water. If the soil has really dried out, the best solution is to immerse it. Submerge the pot in a bucket of lukewarm water and wait until there are no more air bubbles rising to the surface. Be warned, however! The leaves of some plants will droop in very hot weather even though the compost is moist enough. You should move plants like this into the shade for a while.

A lot of container plants form a dense crown of leaves which shade their own pots and prevent rainwater from getting in. You will have to water plants like these even in rainy weather.

Many beneficial
insects will be spared
if you use biological
remedies against pests
and diseases instead
of chemicals
(Fremontodendron
californicum).

Spring and autumn

Spring and autumn (and unfortunately some summers too) can be very wet, and there is a risk that the plants can get too much water. This is why good drainage is so essential. Always make sure that there are holes at the bottom of the container. Put some crocks over the holes to prevent them from becoming plugged up. On top of the crocks you can also add a layer of coarse gravel or expanded clay pebbles, which help excess water to drain away quickly. An added benefit of expanded clay pebbles is that they hold water and release it again slowly in periods of drought.

The leaves of plants in waterlogged soil will droop, just as they will if the soil is too dry.

TIP

If the root ball has dried right out, you should submerge the pot in a bucket of lukewarm water and leave it until air bubbles stop rising to the surface.

46

This is a sign that the roots are no longer taking up moisture because they have rotted. At this point, the plant is almost certainly beyond saving.

Winter Plants that overwinter in a cool place do not need much water. The plant is dormant during this period and is taking up virtually no water for growth. Give the plant just enough water to prevent the root ball from drying out. The finger test is useful here.

Plants that retain their leaves still use a little water for assimilation, but plants that shed their leaves do not even do that any more and may be watered very sporadically. In the early spring, when they start to shoot again, you will need to start watering them more often. It is better to water little but often at this stage, rather than give the plants a real soaking occasionally.

Evergreen plants which overwinter in a warm place - in the house, for instance - simply carry on growing and need watering regularly like all the other house plants.

Water hardness The hardness of tap water varies from one place to another. Your local water company will be able to tell you how hard the water in your area is. Hard water contains a lot of lime. Some plants, like *Camellia* and *Myrtus*, are lime-haters. It is advisable to use rainwater or softened water for these plants. Ericaceous plants (the heathers)

T I P

Always use lukewarm water (approximately 18°C [64°F]) for watering and misting plants in containers - particularly tropical and subtropical plants.

Hedera *(ivy) is an evergreen hardy perennial that will thrive even in dense shade.*

also prefer softer water. *Olea*, on the other hand, likes hard water. If your tap water is soft you can provide additional lime and magnesium. Most other plants are not fussy about the water they get.

Citrus-plants tend to suffer from yellowing leaves. This is usually caused by a deficiency of manganese or magnesium in the soil.

Light and temperature

Light is extremely important to all plants. Most plant species need a few hours of sunlight every day; some rather more, some a little less. This is not really a problem in the summer. You can tailor your collection of container plants to the space you have available and to the light intensity. A great many tropical and subtropical plants will do well on a sunny patio or terrace. In a shady garden you will have to confine yourself to shade-loving or at least shade-tolerant plants.

In winter it is harder to ensure that your plants get enough light. Hardy perennials can simply stay where they are, but frost-tender specimens will have to be found a place indoors. Evergreen container plants, in particular, need a lot of light. A frost-free greenhouse or conservatory is ideal for overwintering this type of plant. A lot of plants can also overwinter very successfully in a cool, light bedroom. You could also, of course, use a cool, dark place and provide artificial lighting, but if you do you must be sure to get special daylight light bulbs. Ordinary light bulbs or fluorescent tubes do not emit light of the right wavelength, and plants will grow weak and spindly. As far as specimen plants are concerned, a rule of thumb is that the higher the temperature is, the more light a plant needs. But if the temperature

Facing page: It takes a lot of patience and skill to grow and train a spiral box like this.

48

gets too high, the plant may be attacked by pests and diseases. In the descriptions of specimen plants (chapter 5), you will find the ideal winter temperature for each type of plant. Specimen plants that lose their leaves in winter can be put in a cool, frost-free place. When you bring them out again in the spring, you will need to protect them from bright sunlight for the first few days, otherwise the leaves can become quite badly scorched. Plants in a greenhouse need to be protected from strong sun even earlier than this. You can do this with greenhouse shading or by painting the glass with shade paint. This will also prevent excessive temperatures early in the season, which would predispose the plants to pests and diseases. Plants which have spent the whole winter outdoors obviously do not need to acclimatize to brighter sunlight and rising temperatures.

If you grow herbs to use in cooking, you should never spray them with chemical pesticides.

Pests and diseases

Plants in containers are rather more susceptible to pests and diseases than plants growing in the open ground. Because of the large fluctuations in temperature and humidity, plants which have to spend the winter indoors are particularly prone to attack by pests like scale insects, aphids and whitefly. On the following pages I have listed the symptoms and probable causes of various pests and diseases, together with suggestions for treating and preventing them. Generally speaking, it is better to start by tackling the problem with biological treatments and only to use chemicals as a last resort.

TIP

Always try to combat pests and diseases by biological means before you resort to chemicals. Beneficial insects like bees and ladybirds will not be harmed and biological remedies are better for the environment.

50

Symptom: young leaves turn yellow, but the veins stay green; later on there is also yellowing of the older leaves.
Cause: iron deficiency as a result of (a) hard water or (b) too much lime in the soil.
Remedy: (a) water with rainwater, softened water or boiledwater; (b) replace compost.

Symptoom: old leaves turn yellow (particularly in *Citrus*).
Cause: magnesium or manganese deficiency.
Remedy: feed with a liquid fertilizer containing extra magnesium and manganese or replace compost.

Symptom: leaves turn yellow with a purplish cast, and very few buds form.
Cause: phosphate deficiency.
Remedy: feed with a liquid fertilizer containing a relatively high proportion of phosphate.

Symptom: all leaves gradually turn light green, then yellow, and growth is stunted.
Cause: nitrogen deficiency.
Remedy: feed with a liquid fertilizer containing a relatively high proportion of nitrogen.

If you sow petunias indoors in early spring you will be able to enjoy a wonderful display from mid-May until late summer.

Symptom: edges of the leaves turn brown and start to curl.
Cause: potash deficiency.
Remedy: feed with a liquid fertilizer containing a relatively high proportion of potash.

Symptom: the plant suddenly drops most of its leaves and buds.
Cause: (a) the soil is becoming waterlogged; (b) the soil is too dry in combination with too high a temperature and insufficient humidity; (c) root pruning.
Remedy: (a) improve the drainage; (b) as the temperature rises, increase the amount of water and raise the humidity by misting regularly; (c) new leaves will shoot from dormant buds once the roots have recovered.

Symptom: brown, fairly round spots on the leaves.
Cause: (a) cold; (b) too much fertilizer; (c) dry fertilizer on the leaves; (d) drops of water on the leaves which cause scorching in the sun; (e) poorly-draining compost.
Remedy: remove affected leaves; (a) bring the plant inside; (b) feed less; (c) avoid spilling fertilizer on leaves; (d) do not spray in the sun; (e) change the compost and add extra sharp sand.

This Diascia *is in full sun. It had to acclimatize to the sun gradually in the spring.*

Symptom:	white, marble-effect patches on the leaves.
Cause:	watering or spraying with water that is too cold.
Remedy:	use lukewarm water.

Symptom:	parchment-like, light brown or dry, white patches on the leaves.
Cause:	too much sun.
Remedy:	protect the plant against fierce midday sun.

Symptom:	widening yellow stripes and mosaic patches on the leaves, misshapen leaves and stunted growth.
Cause:	virus diseases (transmitted by aphids).
Remedy:	destroy the plant.
Comment:	in some variegated *Abutilon* species the mosaic marking is also caused by a virus, but this is harmless to the plant.

Symptom:	red patches on the underside of the leaves (particularly in *Pelargonium* and *Fuchsia*) and misshapen leaves.
Cause:	rust (fungus).
Remedy:	remove and destroy affected parts. Increase the plant's resistance by spraying it with undiluted extract of horse-tail (soak 100 g [4 ozs] of fresh or 50 g [2 ozs] of dried horsetail in 1 litre [2 pints] of water for 24 hours).

The reasonably competent DIY enthusiast will have no difficulty making a square planter like this.

Symptom: tiny red spider-like insects and fine webs.

Cause: red spider mite.

Remedy: destroy severely infested plants. Prevention: spray regularly with a powerful jet of water. In the greenhouse: introduce the parasitic mite Phytoseulis persimilis.

Symptom: notches cut out of leaf edges. No insects visible during the day; small black or dark brown beetles emerge at night. There are whitish larvae in the compost, up to 15 mm (1/2 inch) long.

Cause: vine weevil.

Remedy: spray in the evening with undiluted extract of garlic (soak 50 g [2 ozs] of chopped garlic cloves in 1 litre [2 pints] of water for 24 hours) or place the root ball in lukewarm water for about half an hour until the beetles and larvae float to the top. In both cases replace the compost and wash the roots thoroughly but carefully.

Symptom: holes in leaves and a slimy trail on stems and leaves.

Cause: slugs and snails.

Remedy: remove by hand (slugs hide underneath the pot during the day).

Annuals are fairly easy to propagate from seed.

Comment: new biological and environmentally-friendly remedies are coming on to the market all the time. These are often specifically designed for a particular type of harmful insects, and helpful insects are unaffected by them. Your nursery or garden centre will be able to tell you which remedy is the best for your problem.

Hostas can be divided in spring. Propagate hydrangeas by taking softwood cuttings in June or July.

Propagation   Most plants, even the tropical and subtropical specimen plants, can be propagated fairly easily. You can propagate either by seed (sexually) or vegetatively (asexually) by means of cuttings or division.

Zaaien   Many flowering plants produce seed after flowering in order to reproduce. Try to use the freshest seed you can, since the germination rate of seed diminishes over time. The seed of some species retains the power to germinate much longer than others. Bear in mind that seed you collect yourself from F1 hybrids and some named cultivars will probably not come true. In other words, the seedlings will not be the same as the parent plant. In this case you would do better to buy seed or propagate the plant vegetatively (as I explain below).

If your hobby is breeding new cultivars or hybrids (which can produce some extremely exciting results, particularly in fuchsias), sexual reproduction is the only feasible method. Use special seed and cutting compost, which consists of one part loam, one part river sand, one

Pansies are very happy in a pot.

part clay and some nutrients. Sprinkle the seed carefully on the surface and cover with a thin layer of seed and cutting compost. You should sieve this first, to make sure it is extremely fine. The best time to sow seed is in the spring, when the intensity of the light is increasing. This will promote the strong growth of seedlings and young plants. Once the seedlings are large enough to handle (which usually means when they have formed two real leaves) they can be pricked out. The plants go into ordinary potting compost and are given room to grow on either in separate small pots or spaced some distance apart in a large tray. You will get sturdy, bushy plants by pinching them out. Once the young plants have developed six or more leaves, you should pinch out the youngest (top) pair of leaves. This encourages the plant to produce side shoots. If you want to grow the plant as a standard, do not pinch out the top. Instead, nip out any side shoots that form spontaneously (see also pruning and topiary). Strong plants can be potted on into a decorative pot or combined with other plants in a tub or trough.

Hardening off

Hardy perennials can be sown in trays kept in a cold greenhouse or a sheltered spot outdoors. The young plants can simply stay outside after pricking out. However, if you have grown the plants in a heated greenhouse they will have to be hardened off before you can put them out permanently. For the first two weeks, put the plants out in a shady spot, but only during the day. After this, if there is no risk of night frost they can stay out all night too. Do not put them in the sun until they have had a few weeks to acclimatize to the outside temperatures. Annuals, tropical and subtropical plants usually need a high soil temperature in order to germinate. You can buy special heating mats to go under seed trays, as well as heated propagators in a wide range of sizes. You can also put seed trays on radiators in the house. Whichever method you choose, make sure that the compost remains moist and, if you are not using a propagator, place a sheet of glass or clear plastic over the trays until the seedlings start to appear. As soon as the shoots start to show, remove the glass or plastic or raise it slightly to provide adequate ventilation, otherwise the seedlings can rot or go mouldy (damping off). These plants will also need to be hardened off before they can go out for the summer. The seeds of some tropical and subtropical plants have a hard coating. These should be soaked before they are sown. Leave them in warm water overnight and then plant them up in seed and cutting compost immediately. Allow for the fact that some seeds germinate much more quickly than others. Seeds from one type of plant will germinate within a week, while another plant's seeds can take six months to germinate!

Facing page: A pink Pelargonium *will flower profusely for months so long as you dead head it frequently.*

Cuttings

Many plants can be propagated vegetatively by means of cuttings. This method is often successful with tropical and subtropical

perennials. By taking cuttings, you will get young plants that are exactly like their parents, unlike plants grown from seed. In many cases this will be an advantage - particularly if the parent plant is healthy and flowers abundantly. There are several types of cutting, including stem tip cuttings (or softwood cuttings), semi-ripe cuttings and hardwood cuttings. Heel cuttings are cuttings which are taken with a portion of mature wood (or heel) at the base; and may be semi-ripe or hardwood.

Because Datura *sheds its leaves, it can overwinter in a dark place like a shed or a garage - provided it is frost-free.*

Stem tip cuttings The usual way of taking cuttings is to take stem tip cuttings. Cut off a length of stem with about 6 to 8 pairs of leaves from the tip of a shoot of the parent plant. Remove the lower leaves, but be sure to leave at least two leaves on the stem. Cut the stem off immediately under the junction of the lowest pair of leaves. Keep the wound as small and clean as possible. Dip the end of the cutting into hormone rooting powder and tap off the excess. This powder helps to prevent infections and stimulates root growth. Next, put the cutting into a pot or tray containing seed and cutting compost. Do not push the cutting too far into the compost, but make sure that it is firm. Put the pot or tray in a light place, but not in the sun. Water the compost with a fine rose. To prevent the compost from drying out too quickly, you can cover the pot with a plastic bag. This also helps to give the cutting the right humidity. To prevent mould from forming you will need to turn

Pelargoniums are easy to propagate from cuttings.

the bag inside out every so often, so that the condensation on the inside is then on the outside and can dry. Some species of plants will only root if the soil temperature is high. In this case you can put the pot or tray on a heating mat or in a propagator, or stand it on a radiator. When new leaves appear, this is a sign that the cutting has rooted and you can remove the plastic bag.

Combine annuals and perennials in the same colour range to create a harmonious display.

The water method

A lot of people root stem tip cuttings in a jar of water. Once the cutting has developed roots, it is potted up into ordinary potting compost. This often works quite well, but usually the cutting still has to make new roots first. The roots which the cutting developed in the water are not capable of absorbing nutrients and water from compost. This requires additional energy and time. Another drawback is that these cuttings often die from rot or mould. I therefore recommend the method described in the previous paragraph rather than the water method.Jonge plantjes die uit stekken zijn opgekweekt, moeten net als zaailingen eerst worden afgehard (zie zaaien).

Semi-ripe cuttings

When you take a semi-ripe cutting, you look for a shoot on the parent plant which has already half-ripened. The tip of the shoot is still young and soft, but the bottom is already woody. You sometimes need to leave a heel on the cutting. A heel cutting is taken at the point where the shoot is growing out of the main stem (at the joint). When

you cut it off, you leave a small piece of bark from the main stem attached to the bottom of the cutting. This little piece of bark is known as the heel. The cutting is then treated in exactly the same way as a softwood cutting (see above).

Unlike plants in the open ground, plants in pots - like these Lantana - can be sold all year round.

Hardwood cuttings With a hardwood cutting the shoot is already fully ripe, which means that it will take much longer to root than a softwood cutting. This method is often used for trees and shrubs. Hardwood cuttings generally do not need to be dipped in hormone rooting powder. Hardwood cuttings from hardy trees and shrubs can simply be pushed into the soil outside. This is usually done in the autumn. They will root in the following year and can then be potted up. Hardwood cuttings from tender trees and shrubs will have to be kept inside; some of them need a high soil temperature. Hardwood cuttings are also sometimes taken with a heel (see above).

Young plants grown from cuttings have to be hardened off in the same way as seedlings (see 'sowing seed').

Division Perennials are very often propagated by division. Bushy and clump-forming plants are best suited to this method. The parent plant is removed from the pot (or dug up) and divided into smaller pieces. To divide a plant, hold it by the roots and carefully tear a piece away from the root ball. If it is too tough to do this, you can cut the root ball into pieces using a clean, sharp-edged spade. Make sure that each new piece of plant has roots attached. These pieces can then simply be potted up in the appropriate compost. Water them very thoroughly.

Pruning and topiary

Plants are usually pruned when they get too big, or if there is a lot of dead wood in a tree or shrub. In the latter case it is obvious what has to be cut out, in the former case you will have to think about what you are doing. You need to ensure that you preserve the shape of the plant and that you do not leave any ugly, protruding raw ends. A plant can also be pruned to create a specific, unnatural shape - for instance the balls, pyramids and animal forms often cut in box and yew, or the standard trees created from plants like the marguerite *(Chrysanthemum frutescens)*.

Geometric and animal shapes

It is really not all that difficult to prune a bushy plant into a ball shape. Keep turning the plant all the time you are cutting it so that you keep the shape symmetrical. If you want a pyramid, column or cube, you can use canes and string to show you where to cut. Animal shapes take more experience.

You can make a shape out of chicken wire and place it over a very young plant. Whenever shoots grow outside the wire you can cut them away, carrying on like this until the whole shape has been filled.

The soft pink of the pelargoniums makes a wonderful contrast with the lavender blue of the summer house.

Plants in pots create a charming corner of the patio.

You can then remove the wire, however you can also leave it in place if you prefer. If you let the young leaves grow through the wire, the wire will soon be completely concealed.

Standard tree

To create a standard, start with a young plant that has not been pinched out and has an obvious main stem or leader (see above for pinching out). Whenever a new side shoot appears, cut it away from the main stem. Take care not to remove the leaves that grow on the main stem, because the plant needs them in order to grow. If necessary, you can support the stem with a cane. In most cases the stem will thicken up later on, and will then not need extra support. Once the stem has reached the height you want, it is time to pinch it out. From then onwards, the plant will produce side shoots. In order to get a full, bushy crown, you will have to pinch out the tips of these side shoots too. You can now remove the leaves growing on the main stem below the crown, to get a nice clean look. Once the head is the size you want, all you have to do is prune it all round in the same way as for a ball (see above). Standards are often top-heavy and are therefore prone to being blown over, so it is a good idea to anchor the pot to the ground with metal pins which hook over the edge of the pot.

ou can propagate box (Buxus) by taking hardwood cuttings with a heel in the spring.

Plants for containers

In this chapter I list many of the plants suitable for containers that are available from nurseries and garden centres, with information about the origins, care and propagation of each plant.

Agapanthus *'Midnight Blue'*.

Abutilon

Origin: the genus *Abutilon* has around 150 species originating in South America and Australia, but only a few of them are cultivated. Most of the species are herbaceous, although some can grow into real trees.

As well as the species grown for their ornamental value, there are others grown for the medicinal substances they contain or for the production of -quite strong- fibres. The *Abutilon* was neglected for a while but, happily, is now back in favour as a popular plant for indoor and outdoor containers.

It is occasionally -but erroneously- referred to as the flowering maple.

Description: the many hybrids available come from crosses of *A.*

darwinii and *A. pictum*. They are generally quite robust and well suited to use as a container plant. 'Fireball' has abundant red flowers; 'Cerise Queen' has cherry red flowers; 'Golden Fleece' and 'Lemon Queen' are yellow; 'Boule de Neige' has pure white flowers. *A. megapotamicum* (Belgian flag) has a horizontal growth habit and can also be used as a hanging plant. Yellow petals and almost black stamens protrude from the red, bell-shaped calyx. These are the colours of the Belgian flag - hence the name. *A. megapotamicum* 'Variegatum' has variegated leaves. *A. pictum* 'Thompsonii' has red flowers and, thanks to the *Abutilon* mosaic virus, yellow-splashed green leaves. It is a robust plant which can grow up to 2 metres (6 foot 6 inches) high and lends itself very well to training

as a standard. In its natural habitat, *A. vitifolium* can grow to 7 metres (23 feet) tall. The flowers range from purple to dark blue and are wide open. The leaf is shaped rather like a sycamore leaf. *A. vitifolium* 'White Charm' has white flowers.

Care: *Abutilon* can tolerate a position in full sun, but does better in light shade. It can go outside in mid-May and can stay out until the first night frost. It will overwinter in a warm (20°C, 68°F) or cool (8°C, 45°F) place, but because it is an evergreen it will need plenty of light in either case. Like other house plants, *Abutilons* kept in the warm need watering regularly and should be pruned back hard in the autumn. If the plants are in a cool place, you just need to make sure that the root ball does not dry out. *Abutilon*'s

main flowering period is during the summer months, when it will need additional feeding. Never the spray the plant when the sun is on it, since this can cause ugly scorch marks. *A. vitifolium* has a weak root system and cannot tolerate over-watering.

Pests and diseases: Indoors, *Abutilon* can have problems with whitefly. Stand the plant somewhere out of draughts, and cut an affected plant back hard.

Propagation: *Abutilon* is easy to propagate from cuttings. Take softwood cuttings in spring or semi-ripe cuttings in August. The plant sometimes sets seed, but it is unlikely to come true. By removing the seed heads regularly, you will encourage the plant to produce more flowers.

Agapanthus

Origin: *Agapanthus*, a highly popular, easy-to-grow container plant, came originally from South Africa and is a member of the lily family, hence its common name 'African Lily'.

Description: the *Agapanthus* has long, narrow strap-like leaves, which are usually dark green. The funnel-shaped flowers are borne on stems around 1 metre (39 inches) long, standing well clear of the leaves. They are either blue or white. They also make excellent cut flowers. Some species flower every other year. The species you are most likely to find on sale is *A. praecox*, which has blue flowers. In sheltered areas this could probably even be grown in the open ground, but in

Hybrid Abutilon.

hard winters it would need some additional protection in the shape of dried bracken, pine branches or some other mulch. *A. praecox* 'Alba' is, of course, a white-flowering form. You may well find other *Agapanthus* varieties at the garden centre.

Some specialist nurseries carry a range of very attractive hybrids, like the self-explanatory 'Midnight Blue', which remains small (40 cm, 16 inches), or the free-flowering 'Isis'.

Care: Plant in ordinary potting compost or in a mixture of potting compost and loam or clay. The *Agapanthus* flowers better if it is slightly pot bound, but it outgrows its pot very quickly and has even been known to burst clay pots. The best method, therefore, is to plant it in a plastic inner pot and put this in an ornamental outer container. You do not need to pot on until the plant is growing out of the pot. It prefers a sunny position. Because it is deciduous, it can overwinter successfully in a dark, frost-free garage or shed. It will need virtually no water during this period.

Agapanthus can go outside again in April, and can stay out until October or November. Feed regularly while the plant is in flower, or add a slow-release fertilizer like Osmocote to the compost at the beginning of the season.

Pests and diseases: the *Agapanthus* is effectively trouble-free.

Propagation: the *Agapanthus* responds well to division when you pot it on in the spring. Take care not to cause too much damage to the roots, which are rather delicate. You can grow it from seed, but if you let the plant set seed it will not flower as well the following year. In any event, the seed is unlikely to come true.

Agave

Origin: the *Agave* comes originally from central America. In the fifteenth century, the Spanish conquistadors took it back with them to Spain, where it is now widespread. There are a great many known species, but only a few are cultivated. In tropical and subtropical regions *A. americana* blooms after about ten years,

throwing up flower stalks that are metres high. The parent plant dies off after flowering, but by then will already have produced numerous offspring to keep the species going. The *Agave* is unlikely to flower in a temperate climate, but the thick leaves are extremely decorative. Some *Agave* species are grown for other purposes: *A. sisalana* produces thick fibres, which are used to make the familiar white sisal string, while in Mexico they make a type of wine known as *pulque* from *A. salmiana*.

Description: the *Agave* has narrow, thick, fleshy leaves arranged in a rosette. Water is stored in the leaves, enabling the plant to withstand drought in its natural habitat. It is

Abutilon megapotamicum '*Variegatum*'.

unlikely to flower in our cooler climate. The best known and most widely available species is *A. americana*, which has bluish green leaves that can grow up to 80-120 cm (2 feet 6 inches to 4 feet) long. Popular cultivars include 'Argente-ovariegata' with white-edged leaves; 'Aureovariegata' with pale yellow edges to the leaves, and 'Medio-picta' with yellow stripes along the centre of the leaves. The leaf rosette of *A. filifera* can grow up to 60 cm (2 feet) across. The leaves are green, with a narrow white edge, and they have loose, stringy fibres on the underside. *A. victoriae-reginae* is an attractive and fairly expensive species, which forms rosettes 40 cm (16 inches) wide. The stiff, dark green leaves have white stripes on both the top and the underside, with vicious spines at their tips. One

species that is harder to find is *A. attenuata*, which carries its rosette on a stem that can ultimately grow to 1 m (3 feet) long.

Care: use ordinary potting compost, with the addition of some clay or sharp sand, and give the plant a sunny position in both summer and winter. Water regularly during the summer months. If the plant is allowed to get too dry, the leaves will curl down; however, overwatering will lead to rot. Feed with a liquid fertilizer every two weeks. The *Agave* prefers to overwinter in a light, cool place (about 10°C, 50°F) and requires little water during this period. The sharp spines on the leaves make these plants awkward customers when it comes to moving them or repotting them.

Pests and diseases: the *Agave* is rarely if ever troubled by pests and diseases.

Propagation: From time to time *Agaves* form offshoots around the base of the rosette. These can easily be detached from the parent plant and potted up. *A. victoriae-reginae* is the only species that does not produce offshoots, so that it has to be propagated by seed.

Anisodontea

Origin: *Anisodontea* is a native of South Africa. This plant is currently enjoying renewed popularity - and deservedly so: it bears a profusion of pretty pink flowers all summer long.

Description: *Anisodontea capensis*

Abutilon *'Golden Fleece'*.

Bougainvillea *'Barbara Carst'*.

has deeply lobed leaves, 3-5 cm (1-2 inches) long, with sawtooth edges. The pale pink flowers are quite small (about 2 cm, 3/4 inch) across, but appear in great numbers throughout the growing season. The plant can easily grow into a shrub 1.5 m (5 feet) tall.

Care: *Anisodontea* is very happy in ordinary potting compost, possibly with a little sharp sand added. Feed weekly or every other week during the growing season. The plant can go outdoors after the middle of May, and prefers a sunny position. It must be brought indoors again before the first night frosts and overwinter in a light, cool place (7-12°C, 45-54°F). Cut the water right down. If it is kept any warmer, the plant will soon be prey to aphids and whitefly. Cut the plant back hard before you

bring it in for the winter, to encourage strong bushy growth in the spring.
Because of the plant's bushy habit, it responds well to training as a standard.
Keep on removing any side shoots and let the main stem grow on until it is the height you want.
At this stage, pinch the growing tip out. The plant will then produce side shoots from that point.
Pinch the side shoots out too from time to time, to create a full, bushy top.

Pests and diseases: if the overwintering temperature is too warm, the plant will rapidly succumb to attack by aphids and whitefly. Move it somewhere cooler and, if necessary, push a couple of Plantpins into the compost.

Agave americana '*Aureovariegata*'.

Propagation: *Anisodontea* is easily propagated by means of cuttings, which you can take from the parent plant all summer. Put them in ordinary potting compost mixed with some sand. They will soon root at a soil temperature of around 18°C (65°F).

Bougainvillea

Origin: *Bougainvillea* is a native of Brazil. A specimen was described and named by a botanist in the expedition led by the Frenchman Louis Antoine de Bougainville in the eighteenth century, but the plant was not brought to Europe until the nineteenth century. Nowadays, it

pp. 70-71: Pittosporum tobira.

Agapanthus.

would be impossible to imagine the countries of the Mediterranean without this showy climber. With its superb cascade of floral bracts, *Bougainvillea* can cover large surfaces. In the cooler regions of Europe, *Bougainvillea* is often sold as a house plant, but it does much better as a container plant.

Description: *Bougainvillea* is a climber which uses its curved thorns to cling on to its 'host'. It can grow to quite a height - over 6 m (20 feet) in the open ground. The flowers themselves are small and insignificant. They are white and tubular, and are borne in clusters of three. Each cluster of flowers is surrounded by the brightly-coloured bracts that make this plant so sensational. They are pink, red, purple, white or sometimes yellow.

The species on the market are primarily hybrids, like the crimson-magenta 'Mrs Butt', the cyclamen red 'Amethyst' or the pink 'Barbara Carst'. You will also find many cultivars of *B. glabra* being sold as house plants. The vigorous, pink *B. spectabilis* makes a very good container plant and flowers better than the hybrids.

Care: *Bougainvillea* needs strong supports to climb on, but it can also be grown as a hanging plant. It is happy in ordinary potting compost, but the addition of some clay and bone meal would be appreciated. Feed regularly during the growing season to prevent yellowing of the leaves and eventual leaf drop. It likes a sunny position and flowers profusely on mature wood. Do not prune out too much old wood, since

this will affect flowering. You must bring the plant in before the first night frost. It should overwinter in a cool place. Cut down on watering, giving just enough to ensure that the root ball does not dry right out. *Bougainvillea* is deciduous, so it can overwinter in a dark place, such as a frost-free shed or garage. It can go outside again in the second half of May. If the plant overwinters in a warm living room it will quickly succumb to aphids and red spider mite. The floral bracts are also likely to be much less spectacular next season.

Pests and diseases: if kept too warm in the winter *Bougainvillea* is likely to suffer from red spider mite and aphids. Yellowing of the leaves

Abutilon vitifolium *'White Charm'*.

Agapanthus praecox *'Alba'*.

(chlorosis) may occur during the growing season. This is a sign of nitrogen or iron deficiency.

Propagation: *Bougainvillea* is not easy to propagate. Cuttings, which you can take in the spring, will not ?oot unless the soil temperature is at least 25°C (77°F). Use hormone rooting powder and make sure that the humidity is high.

Brunfelsia

Origin: *Brunfelsia* comes from South America. In their native habitat, some species of this genus are regarded as weeds. Its large, abundant blue-purple flowers make *Brunfelsia* a very popular house plant, but it is fairly difficult to get the plant to bloom again under these conditions. By treating it as a container plant, you are much more likely to get it into flower.

Description: *Brunfelsia calycina* is an evergreen shrub with dark green, lance-shaped leaves. The blue-purple flowers are large (5 cm, 2 inches across) and have a delicious scent. The flower ages through lilac to white, so that three different flower colours can occur on the plant at the same time. *Brunfelsia* is a slow grower and will reach an ultimate height of 60 cm (2 feet).

Care: *Brunfelsia* does not like excessive temperature fluctuations or being moved. In the summer it prefers a sunny position with some light shade during the hottest part of the day. If the temperature rises above 20°C (68°F) you will need to mist the plant regularly. Give it plenty of water and feed regularly during the summer. Because *Brunfelsia* does not have a real dormant period, you should continue to water it regularly and feed it occasionally in the winter. Grow the plant in ordinary potting compost and pot it on every year. Press the compost down firmly and make sure there is a good drainage layer at the bottom of the pot. Prune back lightly at the end of the winter to keep the plant full and bushy.

Pests and diseases: *Brunfelsia* is prone to attack by scale insects.

Propagation: Shoot tip cuttings taken from *Brunfelsia* will only root if you use a hormone rooting powder and the temperature of the compost is at least 25°C (77°F).

Make sure you keep the humidity high.

Buddleja

There are a great many species in the genus *Buddleia* which will grow in the open ground in this country. The best-known, of course, is *B. davidii* (the butterfly bush), which has given rise to a great many cultivars. Its familiar clusters of purple flowers act as a magnet for butterflies in the late summer. However, there are some species that are not really hardy and can consequently only be grown successfully in this country in a container. Of these species, *B. globosa* is the strongest and most suitable for growing as a container plant. This species is native to South America, where it can grow up to 4 m (13 feet) high.

In a container it will not attain anything like this height. *B. asiatica* and *B. crispa* are native to Asia. They are more difficult to grow and are not widely available.

Description: *Buddleia globosa* has grey-green, lance-shaped leaves, with downy hair on the underside. Dense, rounded clusters of fragrant orange flowers are carried in June and July. The equally deliciously scented white flower spikes of *B. asiatica* appear from January to March. This winter-flowering habit makes *B. asiatica* a particularly good subject for a conservatory or winter garden. It can go outdoors in the summer in an out-of-the-way spot. *B. crispa* looks very much like *B. davidii*, but stays much smaller. The lilac racemes appear in late summer.

Care: *Buddleia* is best potted on into ordinary potting compost every year, after which it will require no additional feeding. It likes a sunny position and needs a lot of water in the growing season. Unlike the other *Buddleia* species, *B. globosa* flowers on mature wood, so confine your pruning to the removal of branches that are in the way. The other species flower on the current season's growth and consequently have to be cut back after flowering so that new shoots form.
All *Buddleia* varieties should overwinter in a light place at about 6°C (43°F).

Pests and diseases: this plant can suffer from aphids, but only if it is overwintered at too high a temperature.

Bougainvillea spectabilis.

Agave americana.

Anisodontea capensis.

Propagation: *Buddleia* is easy to propagate by means of semi-ripe cuttings taken in the summer. Plant them in ordinary potting compost. Hormone rooting powder will help.

Callistemon

Origin: *Callistemon* is native to Australia, where it grows in dry areas. In the wild it can grow into a shrub more than 5 m (16 feet) high. There are about twenty-five known species, the most popular for use as a container plant being *C. citrinus*. When the branches of this species are bruised, they give off the lemony scent to which the plant owes its Latin name. The derivation of the plant's common name -bottlebrush- is evident when you see the flowers, since this is exactly what the long, dense spikes resemble.

Description: the evergreen leaves of *Callistemon* are long to lance-shaped. The flowers appear in summer and are carried at the end of a twig in long, dense clusters. The petals and calyxes drop quite quickly, but the striking red stamens are longer-lasting.
The yellow anthers make an eye-catching contrast. The twig simply continues to grow out beyond the inflorescence, and later on new flowers will develop. Where the old flowers were, you will find grey, woody fruit.

Care: *Callistemon* belongs to the Myrtaceae and, like the other members of the family, dislikes lime. It also has very delicate roots, so you should feed with care and be very gentle when potting on (once every three years). It prefers a

potting compost into which some peat, leaf mould or humus-rich loam has been worked. Give it plenty of (softened) water in the summer, and only occasionally a little liquid fertilizer. The root ball must be kept moist, but make sure that the container is free-draining. *Callistemon* is happiest in a warm, sunny position with some protection against the strong midday sun. It can tolerate a slight frost (to -5°C, 23°F). It needs to overwinter in a light, very cool place (no warmer than 5°C, 41°F), and the root ball must never be allowed to dry out. You can prune the plant when you bring it in, but this will affect flowering the following season.

Pests and diseases: *Callistemon* sometimes suffers from yellowing of

75

Cestrum nocturnum.

Cestrum parqui.

p. 83: Citrus limon.

fertilizer. Because it is an evergreen, it must have a light place to over-winter at a temperature of 5-10°C (41-50°F). Water much more sparingly, but do not let the root ball dry out. Some species can withstand a few degrees of frost.

Pests and diseases: *Cistus* is seldom if ever troubled by pests and diseases.

Propagation: seed from *Cistus* hybrids will not come true and in any event is difficult to obtain. Cuttings do not strike readily. You would do better to buy a young plant.

Citrus

Origin: most *Citrus* species come from Asia. They were taken to southern Europe by the Romans and brought from there to more northerly latitudes. *Citrus* became very popular in the seventeenth and eighteenth centuries because of the delicious fruit and because one tree will bear buds, flowers and fruit at the same time. The flowers also have a very pleasant fragrance. It is not clear how many species there are in this genus, and the confusion is compounded by the fact that the experts keep changing the names.

Description: *Citrus* is a shrub or small tree. The oval, evergreen leaves are leathery and slightly glossy. Many *Citrus* species have thorny branches and winged leaf stems. The flowers are usually white, with a strong jasmine-like scent. The plant can bear flower buds, flowers and fruit at one and the same time. The related *Fortunella* (kumquat) is very like its relative and should be cared for in the same way. The small, oval fruits of the kumquat can be eaten peel and all. *Citrus microcarpa* is the result of a cross between *Fortunella* and *Citrus*. It can overwinter at quite high temperatures and is consequently often sold as a house plant. Other advantages are that it remains quite small, and will produce a profusion of flowers and fruit while still young. Most *Citrus* species are grafted on to *Poncirus* (bitter orange), which is sometimes also sold in its own right. This small, reasonably hardy tree is very decorative and strongly resembles *Citrus*.

Care: *Citrus* trees are not particular-ly easy to look after, but the trouble

Cistus aguilari.

Citrus *(orange).*

Datura

Origin: *Datura* (syn. *Brugmansia*) (angel's trumpets) originates from South America. There are two groups in this genus: a group of annuals and a group of perennial shrubs. The latter group includes spectacular flowering plants, which have become very popular in recent years. In the perennials, the trumpet flowers are pendent; the annuals carry them upright and produce large, eye-catching seed pods after flowering.

Description: annual *Datura* is herbaceous. *D. stramonium* can grow to 90 cm (3 feet) tall, and has sharply lobed leaves. The upright trumpet flowers are white or blue.

After flowering, the plant produces large, spiny seed pods containing numerous seeds. *D. stramonium* var. *inermis* has seed pods without spines. All *Datura* are extremely poisonous.

Various species and hybrids of the perennial *Datura* are grown. They all have pendent, trumpet-shaped flowers. *D. suaveolens* has deliciously scented, creamy-white flowers. *D.s.* 'Rosa' has light pink flowers; *D.s.* 'Plena' has a semi-double flower. *D. sanguinea* has orange-red flowers, with are more tubular. *D. rosei* also has tubular flowers, which are yellow-red in colour. The flowers of *D. arborea* are white and smell of vanilla. *D. versicolor* has white flowers. Care: the perennial *Datura* species prefer a very sunny position. They need a great deal of water; on hot,

sunny days they will want as much as a bucketful twice a day. They are also gross feeders and will need a hefty dose of house plant food once a week. *Datura* is very tender and cannot withstand the slightest frost. It prefers to overwinter in a cool, light place (5°C, 41°F), but can stand being in the dark. In this case it will lose its leaves. Cut right down on watering during the dormant period and do not feed the plant. Old plants can be cut back hard in spring. Young plants are best not pruned. Repot *Datura* annually in ordinary potting compost to which you have added some clay or loam, and possibly some well-rotted farmyard manure.

Pests and diseases: *Datura* can have

problems with whitefly and is prone to attack by slugs and snails. If it is not fed well enough, holes will develop in young leaves.

Propagation: *Datura* propagates readily from cuttings. Take slightly ripe softwood cuttings, which will root in either water or compost (at a soil temperature of about 20°C, 68°F). The annual *Datura* species are easy to grow from seed.

Dicksonia

Dicksonia antarctica, the Australian tree fern, can grow many metres tall in its native habitat. It grows relatively slowly in a pot, and will never reach such lofty heights. Its special needs make it a tricky plant to grow.

Description: *Dicksonia*'s much-divided fronds have yellow veins. They can grow up to 1 m (3 feet) long. After some years, a stem forms under the leaf rosette.

Care: *Dicksonia antarctica* can tolerate a slight frost. It overwinters most successfully at 10°C (50°F). It needs high humidity and a shady position all year round. Mist twice a day in summer. This plant really does better in a greenhouse or conservatory, where you can keep the humidity higher. Use free-draining, humus-rich soil.

Pests and diseases: *D. antarctica* is prone to attack by scale insects. If the air is too dry, the leaves will turn brown.

Propagation: *D. antarctica* forms offsets and spores in the spring. Although it is not an easy job, you can propagate the plant from these offsets.

Eriobotrya

Origin: *Eriobotrya japonica* (loquat) is native to China and Japan. This tree is also widely planted in warm areas south of the Alps. The orange-yellow fruits look like apricots and have a sweet, refreshing taste. The loquat can tolerate slight frost and can be grown outdoors in a well-sheltered spot, but it is safer to treat it as a container plant.

Description: *Eriobotrya japonica* is a slow-growing evergreen fruit tree.

Convolvulus cneorum.

Datura suaveolens (Brugmansia).

Clianthus puniceus.

p. 89: Hedychium ellipticum.

The undersides of the long leaves are downy. The fragrant, pale yellow flowers are borne in clusters, but in the colder parts of the country the plant will rarely if ever flower. It is more likely to flower in a greenhouse and, if you want fruit, you will have to pollinate it artificially.
Some species are not self-pollinating, which means that another individual is needed.

Care: plant *Eriobotrya* in ordinary potting compost with some sharp sand, and make sure there is good drainage. Since the plant is relatively frost hardy it need not be brought inside until quite late in the year. Put it in a light place at a temperature between 10 and 20°C (50 and 68°F). Do not mist the plant.

Pests and diseases: *Eriobotrya* does not like a lot of rain or spray. It is susceptible to fire blight and moulds which cause rot and fungal leaf spot.
Propagation: *Eriobotrya japonica* can be raised from seed. It is almost impossible to propagate it from cuttings.

Erythrina

Origin: *Erythrina* (coral tree) comes originally from South America and South Africa. The genus is a member of the Leguminosae family. A number of species are cultivated and these are relatively easy to grow. The exotic flowers create a stunning effect.

Description: the winter-flowering *Erythrina caffra* and *E. lysistemon* can grow to as much as 7 m (23 feet)

in their natural habitat, but obviously they will remain much smaller when confined to a pot. *E. crista-galli* has a short, thick trunk with long, straight branches. It flowers on new wood. The long trusses of scarlet flowers appear in the summer. *E. crista-galli* 'Compacta' flowers as a very young plant. The shoots on this cultivar do not grow as long.

Care: plant *Erythrina* in ordinary potting compost with some well-rotted manure and one-third clay. Make sure that the drainage is good, for instance by adding some sharp sand. The plant is tender, so it cannot go outside until the middle of May. It prefers a sunny position. Feed regularly and remove dead flower heads to prolong the flowering season. It will have to be

Alyogyne huegelii *'Trumpet Serenade'*
(see: Hibiscus*)*.

Hibiscus *'Boondah'*.

brought back inside relatively early. Make sure that the root ball is dry when you bring it in. It can overwinter in a cool, dark place, where it will require very little water. Repot in spring and cut out any dead wood close to the trunk.

Pests and diseases: *Erythrina* is seldom if ever troubled by pests and diseases.

Propagation: you can propagate *Erythrina* by seed or by taking cuttings in spring. You should take young shoots about 10 cm (4 inches) long with a heel, and root them at a soil temperature of about 25°C (77°F).

Eucalyptus

Origin: in its native habitat of

Australia, there are more than 500 known species of *Eucalyptus*. Only three of them are suitable for growing in containers. *Eucalyptus* is known primarily for the medicinal oils obtained from the leaves. Koalas live exclusively on *Eucalyptus* leaves, which is why these little creatures have such a distinctive smell.

Description: all *Eucalyptus* species are heterophyllous, in other words they have different leaves when young and when they are older. *E. gunnii* initially has small, round, bluish grey leaves, often borne in bunches. Later the leaves become elongated. It is a strong plant, which can flower in this country. The unusual flowers are white, with conspicuous stamens. *E. globulus* has white-tinged, blue-grey leaves

and seldom comes into flower. The leaves of *E. citriodora* are lemon-scented. The bark is white, with a hint of pink. All three are very vigorous, but pruning will keep them in check.

Care: plant *Eucalyptus* in a mixture of two parts ordinary potting compost to one part clay. Older plants should only be repotted once every eight to ten years. The plant can go outdoors in the second half of May, and prefers a warm, sunny position. Keep well watered, but make sure that drainage is good, because if the root ball becomes waterlogged the roots will rot. You can cut the plant back hard before you bring it in again. This evergreen plant needs a light and fairly cool place (no more than 10°C, 50°F) to overwinter. Give it just enough water to prevent the root ball from drying right out.

Pests and diseases: virtually none.

Propagation: cuttings do not strike readily. *Eucalyptus* can be grown from seed at a soil temperature of about 25°C (77°F).

Felicia

Origin: *Felicia amelloides,* the blue marguerite, is a native of South Africa. This small shrub is covered with charming, daisy-like flowers all summer. Often sold as an annual, *Felicia* can be kept going very successfully.

Description: *Felicia* has narrow

Datura suaveolens.

grey-green leaves. It is a shrub with a bushy habit. The blue flower heads have bright yellow centres, and the plant flowers from early May to autumn. When well cared-for, *Felicia* can grow to 1 m (3 feet) high. You can turn it into a standard, although not a very tall one because the stem is so slender.

Care: *Felicia* can be grown in ordinary potting compost. Water regularly and feed every other week during the growing season. It prefers a sunny position, but half-shade will not do it any harm. *Felicia* is frost tender and must be brought inside before the first night frost.
It needs a light place and an average temperature of about 10°C (50°F) to overwinter.

Pests and diseases: virtually none.

Propagation: *Felicia* is easy to propagate from cuttings. You are more likely to succeed if you take a cutting with a heel. Put the cuttings in special seed and cutting compost. By pinching out the tops regularly, you will ensure that the plants stay compact and bushy.

Fremontodendron

Origin: *Fremontodendron californicum* is a magnificent shrub or tree from California and Mexico, where it can grow up to 5 m (16 feet) high and will flower all year round. In temperate regions it can grow just as tall, provided it is grown against a south-facing wall, but will only flower in the summer months. In severe winters it will require

Convolvulus mauritanicus.

protection with pine branches, bracken or some other mulch.

Description: *Fremontodendron* is an evergreen shrub. The leaves are not unlike fig leaves and are covered with tiny rust-brown hairs that can cause an allergic reaction. The saucer-shaped flowers are bright yellow and are very popular with bumble bees. It responds well to being trained. Two very attractive cultivars are available: 'California Glory' and 'Pacific Sunset'.

Care: *Fremontodendron californicum* likes a sunny position in summer and winter alike. Water regularly during the growing season and provide good drainage. It will appreciate an occasional feed and is amenable to being pruned

into shape. Bring young plants in before the first frost and overwinter them at a temperature of 5-8°C (41-46°F).

Pests and diseases: virtually none.

Propagation: propagation by cutting is not easy. *Fremontodendron* can be raised from seed, but seeds are hard to come by.

Fuchsia

Origin: the *Fuchsia* is a very well-known pot plant. The shrub is indigenous to Central and South America, where more than a hundred species grow. An amazing number of cultivars and hybrids have been developed, and the end is by no means in sight.

Datura suaveolens.

Description: in most *Fuchsia* cultivars the leaves are opposed in pairs. The flowers appear in the leaf joints of the long, oval leaves. The flowers are generally pendent, but there are a few cultivars with upright flowers. In *Tryphylla* hybrids the flowers hang in clusters. The flower tube is quite long, with four sepals. Inside this there are four petals (in double varieties there are more), the long stamens and the even longer stigma. The sepals and petals are usually different colours. After flowering, *Fuchsias* may produce cylindrical fruits, which can be red, purple or green.

Care: *Fuchsias* were originally forest plants, so they prefer partial shade and fairly high humidity.

Iochroma coccineum.

Hibiscus '*Swan Lake*'.

The flowers will last much better in these conditions than they will in full sun. Place them in a sheltered spot out of the wind and mist them regularly. They are perfectly happy in ordinary potting compost, but you can add some leaf mould or clay if you wish. Water daily and feed every week. Stop feeding in mid-August and gradually reduce the amount of water. The plants can be cut back hard before they go away for the winter. Young plants that have not become woody are best overwintered at a moderately high temperature (10-15°C, 50-60°F), so that they continue to grow. Water these plants regularly and feed them occasionally.

Older *Fuchsias* overwinter most successfully in a greenhouse with an average temperature of around 8°C (46°F). They can also be kept in a

dark place, in which case they will lose their leaves and require very little water.

You can also bury *Fuchsias* if you wish. Find a fairly dry spot in the garden and dig out a hole in which you can lay the plants (not in their pots). Cover with peat and place a piece of expanded polystyrene over the top. Put laths and a piece of plastic on top and cover the whole thing with the earth excavated from the hole.

Get the plants out of the pit in March and gradually acclimatize them to higher temperatures and more light.

Do not prune until spring.

Pests and diseases: *Fuchsias* are prone to attack by red spider mite, whitefly, aphids and rust. Remove any leaves affected with rust and

burn them. Clean your tools thoroughly.

Propagation: *Fuchsias* are easy to propagate by means of cuttings. If you want to train a standard, take stem tip cuttings in early September. For bushy plants you can take stem tip or side shoot cuttings throughout the season. Pinch out the young plants and also pinch out the tips of the side shoots several times.

Grevillea

Origin: around two hundred species in the genus *Grevillea* have been described. They originally occurred only in Australia, where some species can grow into huge trees. In the northern hemisphere, *G. robusta* (silky oak) is available as a container plant. It will not get as

93

Mandevilla suaveolens.

Mandevilla 'Aphrodite'.

sold as an annual, but it can be kept from one season to the next quite successfully. The flowers have a lovely fragrance, particularly in the evening, and butterflies find them irresistible.

Description: the leaves of *Heliotropium arborescens* (heliotrope) are dark green and finely wrinkled. The plant is covered in downy hair. The small flowers, which cover the plant in dense, flat clusters all summer, range from dark purple to lavender. They have a strong vanilla scent.

Care: *Heliotropium* likes humus-rich soil, for example ordinary potting compost with added leaf mould. It benefits from a little lime in the compost. Repot the plant annually and make sure it has good drainage. During the growing season, feed the plant from time to time and give it some blood and bone meal. Young plants should be pinched out and lightly pruned regularly to keep them compact and bushy. You can also train *Heliotropium* to create a standard. The plant is frost tender and must be brought inside before any danger of frost. Leave it to overwinter in a light place at a temperature of around 10-15°C (50-60°F) and water only occasionally.

Pests and diseases: whitefly may occasionally be a problem.

Propagation: *Heliotropium* is easy to propagate from seed or by taking cuttings. In both cases the soil temperature will need to be around 20°C (68°F).

Hibiscus

Origin: the genus *Hibiscus* comprises hundreds of species, which are found in virtually every tropical and subtropical region of the world. Some species can grow into real trees. The best known as a container plant is *H. rosa-sinensis*; there are some magnificently flowering hybrids which are widely available.

Description: the dark green leaves of the *Hibiscus* are oval, tapering to a point, and toothed. The funnel-shaped flowers of *H. rosa-sinensis* hybrids are often brightly coloured and fairly large. They are borne all summer long. The hybrid 'Cooperi' has a pink leaf, flecked with green, and small red flowers. Single- and double-flowering hybrids are also

available. The flowers of *H. schizopetalus* are really spectacular: the calyx is tubular and the red, deeply serrated petals are reflexed.
The elongated stamens and pistil are borne high above the flower.
H. landerii has red flowers with finely wrinkled petals. *H. huegelii* (syn. *Alyogyne huegelii*) has large flowers ranging from sky-blue to lavender.

Care: the *Hibiscus rosa-sinensis* cultivars prefer a warm, sunny position in summer. Try to avoid moving the plant if you possibly can, since changing its position can cause bud drop. It will also drop buds and leaves if it is kept short of water. Pot *Hibiscus* on every spring into fresh, general purpose potting compost, to which you can add some clay if you wish, and feed it

every other week. The plant must be brought inside before the first night frost. It will overwinter most happily in a light, fairly cool place (10-15°C, 50-60°C). Be sure to keep the root ball moist. *H. schizopetalus* and *H. huegelii* need to be kept very warm in summer, so it is wise to bring them inside if the weather is cold and wet. *H. huegelii* is relatively drought-resistant and consequently needs less water than the other two species. *H. schizopetalus* and *H. huegelii* can overwinter in the living room, but you will have to mist them regularly. They can be trained to form a standard.

Pests and diseases: *Hibiscus* can sometimes suffer from chlorosis (yellowing of the leaves). Give it some lime and fertilizer. It is also

prone to attack by whitefly, red spider mite and aphids.

Propagation: Take stem tip cuttings in spring and root them at a soil temperature of about 25°C (77°F).

Iochroma

Origin: *Iochroma* comes from Central and South America, where it can grow into a large shrub up to 2.5 m (8 feet) tall. Three species are cultivated, all of which produce pretty tubular flowers in profusion in July and August.

Description: *Iochroma* has fairly large, long leaves. If kept in a warm temperature during the winter it is

Well-tended plants will reward you with a profusion of flowers.

evergreen. The tubular flowers are borne in dense clusters at the tip of a branch. The flowers of *I. coccineum* are a light red, *I. cyaneum* has flowers ranging from lilac to purple, and *I. grandiflorum* has trumpet-shaped flowers in shades of light to dark blue.

Care: *Iochroma* is a member of the same family as the *Datura*, and requires the same care. This means that you will have to give it plenty of water and fertilizer. Pot the plant on every year. If necessary you can prune the roots and cut the branches back lightly. *Iochroma* can be grown as a standard.

Pests and diseases: whitefly and red spider mite can sometimes be troublesome. Grey mould may be a problem in cold, wet summers.

Propagation: take stem tip cuttings during the summer.

Jasminum

Origin: the great majority of the *Jasminum* species (true jasmine) come from Asia. Some of the species, like the winter-flowering *J. nudiflorum* (winter jasmine), are fully hardy but most are frost tender. The climbing species are particularly suited to use as container plants. The flowers of many of the jasmine species are highly fragrant and these plants are widely grown for the production of perfume. In the area around Grasse, the perfume capital of France, whole fields have been planted with jasmine.

Description: *Jasminum* has fairly

Passiflora violacea.

small, long and highly glossy leaves. *J. officinale* has small, deliciously fragrant white flowers; the flowers of the cultivar *J.o.* 'Grandiflorum' are also white and equally fragrant, but larger. The flowers of *J. poly-anthum* are pink on the outside; *J. beesianum* has dark pink flowers and the flowers of *J.* x *stephanense* are pale pink. They are quite vigorous climbers, requiring a large pot and sturdy support.

Care: all *Jasminum* species can be taken outside fairly early in spring. If there is a night frost, they will need protection with rush matting or plastic bubble film. They have a very vigorous growth habit and are happiest in a large pot with fertile soil (potting compost with extra

Oxypetalum caeruleum

Passiflora caerulea.

fertilizer and some added clay). Feed plants every other week in the summer. They prefer a sunny position, but will tolerate light shade. Do not bring them in too early in the autumn, since this will have an adverse effect on flowering next season. Make sure that the root ball is not too wet when you bring the plant in; if it is, the branches may die back. Overwinter the plants in a light, cool place (5-10°C, 41-50°F).

Pests and diseases: *Jasminum* is essentially trouble-free.

Propagation: take stem tip cuttings in summer and root them at a soil temperature of about 20°C (68°F). You can also propagate by layering. Do this by bending a twig down until it touches the soil and partially covering it with soil. After a while, roots will form on the section that is underground. At this point you can cut the twig away from the parent plant and pot up the new plant.

Lantana

Origin: *Lantana camara* is a native of South America, where it can grow into a shrub 2 m (8 feet) tall. It is often sold as an annual, but can be overwintered very success- fully, and with a little patience you can grow it from a small bedding plant into a full-sized shrub, smothered in flowers. *Lantana* has also been introduced into Africa, where it has become a weed which is being eradicated by all possible means. Since it is frost tender, the plant will never cause these problems in temperate regions.

Description: *Lantana* has elongated, oval leaves with rough hairs on the surface. They give off a fairly pungent smell if bruised. In the species, the orange-yellow flowers age to brownish-red. Many cultivars have been developed over the years, with colours ranging from white and yellow to pink and lilac. The unripe fruit which appear after flowering are poisonous and should be removed. This will also encourage the production of more flowers. *Lantana camara* can be trained quite easily to form a standard.

Care: *Lantana camara* prefers a warm, sunny position on the patio during the summer. It needs a great deal of water and organic fertilizer. It is a good idea to pinch out the growing tips several times to keep

Pelargonium-*hybrids.*

Zantedeschia aethiopica.

Pag. 101: Nerium oleander.

the plant full and bushy. To prolong the flowering period you must remove the dead flower heads regularly. Bring *Lantana* inside before the first night frost. You can cut the plant back hard at this time. If you keep it in a light, moderately cool place (about 10°C, 50°F) and water it occasionally, it will carry on flowering right through the winter. In a cooler, light place (5-10°C, 41-50°F) it will stop flowering but will retain its leaves. In a dark place it will lose its leaves, but will simply produce new shoots in the spring. Give it much less water during the dormant period than during spring and summer.

Young plants should be potted on every year; old plants every 3-5 years. *Lantana* is happy in ordinary potting compost, perhaps with some added humus.

Pests and diseases: whitefly can be a real problem. Make sure that the plant is not standing in a draught.

Propagation: *Lantana* can be raised from seed, although seed you collect yourself will not come true. It can also be propagated by means of stem tip cuttings, which you should take in spring.

Laurus

Origin: *Laurus nobilis*, the bay laurel or sweet bay, is indigenous to the countries of the Mediterranean, where this evergreen shrub or tree can grow to over 10 m (35 feet) high. The insignificant, pale yellow flowers only appear on older specimens and it is therefore grown primarily for its aromatic foliage. The dried leaves are widely used in

cooking to impart a delicious aroma and flavour to all sorts of dishes. Bay is one of the staple herbs in a *bouquet garni*. The ancient Greeks made laurel wreaths from the leaves as a symbol of honour and glory.

Description: *Laurus* is a slow-growing shrub or small tree. The young leaves are light green, darkening as they age. They are leathery and slightly glossy. The trunk will turn a very dark brown to almost black. The plant is dioecious. Males bear pale yellow flowers with stamens only. Female plants produce small flowers which only have pistils, which develop into small oval fruit after fertilization. The bay tree seldom flowers in this country.

Care: *Laurus nobilis* thrives in

(25-30°C, 77-86°F), preferably twice a day. Since *Nerium* likes warmth and sunlight, it is difficult to get it to bloom as well as it does in its natural habitat. Further north, the spring nights are really too cold for the plant to set buds. You should consequently put the plant outside as early in the year as possible, but bring it in again in the evening. *Nerium* is a gross feeder. Give it extra fertilizer during the growing season, preferably little and often rather than a lot at one go. If you want to encourage plenty of flowers it is better not to feed too much in spring. A good growing medium is also important. Take ordinary potting compost and add some clay or loam, well-rotted farmyard manure and sharp sand, and some

bone meal. Oleanders like to be in a big pot. Repot young plants every year, older plants every three years. Oleanders often become bare underneath. To prevent this, you should prune the plant back hard before it goes to its winter quarters. Oleanders prefer to overwinter in a light, cool place (4-8°C, 39-46°F). It can withstand brief periods of frost (to -5°C, 23°F) provided that the root ball is dry. Water sparingly and do not feed.

Pests and diseases: aphids, scale insects and red spider mite can be troublesome. In wet summers, in particular, the plant is prone to attack by a fungus. The leaves and young shoots wilt and brown patches appear in the leaf joints. Move the plant immediately to a spot that is out of the rain. Cut all

affected parts out of the plant and then disinfect your secateurs or pruning knife immediately with a 96% alcohol solution. Another troublesome complaint is a bacterial canker known as oleander canker. An affected plant will develop wart-like, dark brown cankers on the stems and sometimes light, watery patches on the foliage. Cut out all the affected parts and burn them. If the attack is really severe you will have to destroy the whole plant. In any event isolate the plant and protect it from cold and damp. Again, you will need to disinfect your secateurs thoroughly.

Propagation: *Nerium* is quite easy to propagate from cuttings. Take softwood cuttings in the summer

Felicia amelloides.

Felicia amelloides.

and pot them up in individual pots. Hormone rooting powder can be helpful.

Olea

Origin: it is not clear where the *Olea* (olive) originally came from. The plant has been under cultivation for so long and so many subspecies and cultivars have been developed that it is difficult to pinpoint its origins. In any event it is a common crop plant in the countries of the Mediterranean, where it is grown for the production of large quantities of olives and olive oil. It takes 10 to 15 years for an olive tree to start bearing fruit, but once it does it will remain productive for decades. Description: In Mediterranean countries *Olea europea* grows into

a tree 10 m (33 feet) high with an irregularly shaped top. It has narrow, silver-grey leaves. It grows very slowly and takes many years to come into flower for the first time. The tiny, fragrant flowers are an off-white colour. The olives develop after flowering. They are stone fruits with a large stone.

Care: *Olea europea* makes a fairly amenable container plant. It can tolerate drought and will not come to any harm if you occasionally forget to water it. The olive will be quite happy in a general purpose potting compost, provided you give it a little added lime every now and again. Repot young plants every year and older plants every two years. Make sure the container is well drained. Put *Olea* in a sunny, warm position on the patio. In order

Trachelospermum jasminoides.

to get fruit you will need either two plants or a self-fertile cultivar. Feed regularly during the growing season with a liquid house plant fertilizer. *Olea* can overwinter in the house, but must have a very light position. Water normally but do not feed. In a cooler place, it will need less water.

Pests and diseases: *Olea* is virtually untroubled by pests and diseases.

Propagation: take cuttings of this year's wood; provide a high soil temperature (25-30°C, 77-86°F) and use a plastic bag to keep the humidity up.

Oxypetalum

Origin: *Oxypetalum caeruleum*

109

Hybrid Pelargonium.

Solanum rantonnetti

p. 111: Hedychium coccineum.

(syn. *Tweedia caerulea*) is a herbaceous climber from South America. It will not grow more than 1 m (3 feet) high. It is often sold as an annual but can be kept quite successfully from year to year. The flowers are very striking, since they change colour as they mature.

Description: *Oxypetalum caeruleum* is a small climber with heart-shaped, hairy leaves. The fragrant tubular flowers are initially light blue. As they age, they change colour to green and then to purple. Just before they wither, they turn lilac. If you dead head the plant regularly, it will keep on flowering until well into the autumn.

Care: *Oxypetalum* thrives in ordinary potting compost with extra sharp sand added. It prefers a sunny position. Give it plenty of water and mist regularly during the summer months. Feed with a house plant fertilizer weekly. Bring the plant inside early and leave it to over-winter in a cool, light place (about 7°C, 45°F). Prune in spring and pinch out the side shoots regularly.

Pests and diseases: aphids can be a problem.

Propagation: sow seed in spring at a soil temperature of 20°C (68°F) or take softwood cuttings, which will root at this same soil temperature.

Passiflora

Origin: most of the over 400 *Passiflora* species are indigenous to America, but there are some which come from Asia or Australia. One species is grown for its edible fruit, the rest for their great ornamental value. *Passiflora* (passion flower) has large, exotic blooms which, according to the first missionaries in America, symbolize the passion of Christ. The ten sepals and petals represent the ten good apostles (Peter, who denied Jesus, and Judas, who betrayed him, are excluded), the three styles depict the three nails with which Christ was nailed to the cross and the ovary is seen as the sponged soaked in vinegar. The best known of the species is *P. caerulea*, which is often sold as a house plant but also makes an excellent container plant.
If you can give it a sheltered position against a south-facing wall it will even survive in the open ground.

Trachelospermum jasminoides.

Heliotropium arborescens.

to the date palm, *P. dactylifera*, which grows too large to be practicable in a container. You also need a male and at least one female in order to get fruit. *P. canariensis* can also get tall and very broad, but it is slower-growing. *P. roebelenii* is another member of the family - this time from Laos. It is much smaller, only growing to about 2 m (6 feet) tall -hence its common name of miniature or pygmy date palm- but it is harder to grow and requires a great deal more care and attention than *P. canariensis*.

Description: *Phoenix canariensis* has feather-shaped, arching leaves, which can be very sharp. It is an evergreen.
In time, a sturdy, fibrous trunk forms underneath. The roots of this palm have a tendency to climb out

of the pot, which makes repotting essential.

Care: in summer, *P. canariensis* likes a warm, sunny position. When it is first brought out from its winter quarters, you should stand it in the shade for a while, before moving it into full sun, otherwise the leaves may be scorched. It can be repotted in spring, and the roots can be pruned at this time without any problem. Grow *Phoenix* in ordinary potting compost with a lot of additional clay or loam and some sharp sand. Older specimens need repotting once every three or four years. *P. canariensis* can tolerate a slight frost, but *P. roebelenii* is extremely tender and even in August the nights can already be too cold for it! *P. canariensis* should overwinter in a cool, light place (4-8°C, 39-46°F). *P. roebelenii*

needs to be somewhat warmer, and they both want high humidity.
If space is a problem, you can tie the foliage up.

Pests and diseases: overwatering will cause root rot, and red spider mite may be a nuisance.

Propagation: you can raise *Phoenix* from seed at a soil temperature of about 25°C (77°F), but be prepared for a wait - germination is very slow.

Phormium

Origin: there are many *Phormium* cultivars available. They are all derived from two species, *P. tenax* and *P. colensoi*, which are native to New Zealand and give the plant its common name of New Zealand flax.

114

They make very attractive container plants, creating a real Mediterranean feel on a patio or terrace.

Description: *Phormium* resembles a grass. The bold, sword-shaped foliage is very robust and varies in colour depending on the cultivar. 'Purpureum' and 'Rubrum' have reddish-brown foliage, 'Aureum' has green leaves with yellow stripes, and the leaves of 'Variegatum' are also green, but with a red border and vertical white stripes. The leaves of *P. tenax* can grow as long as 2.5 m (8 feet), but *P. colensoi* stays much smaller (up to 1 m or 3 feet). New Zealand flax blooms sporadically. The flowers are borne in long, loose panicles and are red or yellowish.

Care: *Phormium* is happy in full sun or partial shade during the summer. *P. tenax* needs a fair amount of water, *P. colensoi* much less. Grow the plant in ordinary potting compost and feed sparingly once every two or three weeks. There is no need to repot until the plant becomes too big for its container. You can take this opportunity to divide the plant into smaller pieces. *Phormium* is reasonably hardy, but will not stand frost for a prolonged period. Because it is evergreen, it needs a light place to overwinter. The temperature should remain between 4 and 10°C (39-50°F). Cut right back on water during the winter.

Pests and diseases: virtually none.

Propagation: propagate *Phormium* by dividing larger plants. Use a

Magnolia grandiflora.

sharp spade to cut through the roots. It is difficult to grow from seed.

Pistacia

Origin: *Pistacia lentiscus* and *P. terebinthus* originally come from Portugal. *P. vera* (the true pistachio nut) is a native of the Middle East. This is the source of the well-known pistachio nuts, which are eaten roasted and salted, and also used to make ice cream and liqueur. *P. terebinthus* provides the raw material for turpentine. Some of the cultivars of *P. lentiscus* are the source of raw materials for toothpaste, chewing gum, and resin used in the manufacture of varnish.

Fuchsia-*hybrids*.

Description: *Pistacia* is a shrub or small tree with attractively glossy, leathery leaves composed of oval leaflets.

The plant is dioecious so a female specimen will only produce berries if there is a male in the vicinity. *P. lentiscus* is evergreen, the other two species are deciduous.

Care: plant *Pistacia* in a deep pot, using ordinary potting compost with some added clay or loam, and make sure it is very free-draining. Repot older plants every three years. *Pistacia* likes a position in full sun during the summer. It is extremely drought tolerant. It can stand a certain amount of frost, so does not have to be brought in early in the autumn. Put the evergreen species

in a cool, light place (1-5°C, 34-41°F); the deciduous varieties can be put somewhere dark. Water very sparingly during the dormant period.

Pests and diseases: *Pistacia* is effectively free of pests and diseases.

Propagation: grow from seed at a soil temperature of 20-25°C (68-77°F). You can take cuttings, but they do not root easily.

Pittosporum

Origin: the genus *Pittosporum* includes a number of cultivated species which do extremely well in a pot or tub. *P. crassifolium*, *P. tenuifolium* and *P. undulatum* are natives of New Zealand and

Fuchsia *hybrids* and Pelargonium *hybrids*.

Australia. *P. tobira*, which can tolerate temperatures as low as -10°C (14°F), comes from East Asia. A number of attractive cultivars with variegated foliage are widely available.

Description: *Pittosporum* is an evergreen. The leaves of *P. crassifolium*, like the young twigs, are grey-felted on the underside. The flowers are dark red. *P. tenuifolium* has light green, wavy-edged leaves and dark-coloured twigs.

The dark red flowers are strongly fragrant, particularly in the evening. The dark green foliage of *P. tobira* is thick and leathery. The white, waxy flowers appear early in spring and are pleasantly scented.

P. undulatum has fairly large, leathery leaves and very fragrant, pendent white flowers.

Care: grow *Pittosporum* in ordinary potting compost to which you can add some clay if you wish. Repot the plant every 3 to 5 years. At the same time you can cut back the root ball. The plant is also amenable to pruning above ground - in fact, pruning is essential in order to achieve strong, bushy growth.
Pittosporum does well in partial shade and is reasonably drought-tolerant. The plant needs to overwinter in a light, fairly cool place.

Pests and diseases: scale insects and aphids can sometimes be troublesome.

Propagation: take softwood cuttings and root them at a soil temperature of about 25°C (77°F). *Pittosporum* can also be raised from seed.

Plumbago

Origin: there are twenty known species of the genus *Plumbago*, but only one is cultivated.
P. auriculata, originating from South Africa, is often sold as a house plant, but it does much better as a container plant.
It has one slightly irritating habit - as they die, the flowers become sticky and will cling to the clothes of anyone passing by.

Description: *Plumbago* is a scrambling climber with long, weak stems which need support. It can grow up to 3 m (10 feet) tall, but is

very amenable to pruning. The light green leaves are oval to elliptic. The primrose-like flowers are borne in trusses and are the most wonderful sky-blue. *Plumbago* will flower throughout the summer, particularly if you dead head the plant regularly. If *Plumbago* is planted in an open bed in a greenhouse or conservatory it can even bloom all year round. *P.a.* 'Alba' has white flowers.

Care: *Plumbago* prefers a sheltered, sunny spot. Give it a large pot and plant it in ordinary potting compost with the addition of extra humus and clay or loam. Water well during the summer, but make sure the compost is well-drained. An occasional feed with house plant fertilizer will be gratefully received.

Solanum jasminoides *'Album'*

Pittosporum tobira 'Variegata'

Plumbago auriculata.

p. 119: Hedychium forrestii.

You can cut the plant back quite hard before you bring it inside. During the winter keep *Plumbago* in a cool place (5-10°C, 41-50°F). If the root ball is kept fairly dry and the light levels are low, the foliage will shrivel.
This is not a cause for concern. Move the plant to a lighter position in early spring and gradually start giving it more water, and it will certainly start to shoot again and produce new leaves.

Pests and diseases: *Plumbago* may have problems with red spider mite if it is overwintered at too high a temperature.

Propagation: take stem tip cuttings in spring or autumn and root them at a soil temperature of about 20°C (68°F).

Podocarpus

Origin: there are a number of species in the *Podocarpus* genus, some of which are hardy in this country. *P. macrophyllus*, however, is not, and consequently has to be grown in a pot.
This evergreen species is native to Japan.

Description: *Podocarpus* has needle-like foliage which remains on the plant all year round. It can be pruned into all sorts of shapes, like the familiar *Taxus* (yew), but it grows slowly, so it will be some time before you achieve the shape you want.

Care: grow *Podocarpus* in ordinary potting compost with some added clay, and give it some extra fertilizer every two weeks during the summer. This plant will do well in sun or shade. It can tolerate a certain amount of cold in the winter, but will have to be brought inside during periods of severe or persistent frost. Put it in a cool, light place. It can go outside again quite early in the spring, but take care that new young shoots do not get nipped by the frost.

Pests and diseases: virtually none.

Propagation: take softwood cuttings in July or August and root them under plastic at a soil temperature of about 25°C (77°F).

Podranea

Origin: *Podranea* is a South African climber with a lovely, tropical look.

118

Punica granatum.

Tecomaria capensis.

bright scarlet. The plant comes into bloom early in the summer and the flowers stay on the plant until well into the autumn. The plant is evergreen.

Care: *Russelia* hates having wet feet, so free-draining compost is essential. Use ordinary potting compost and add extra sharp sand. Water little but often, and feed with house plant food occasionally. It prefers a sunny position. Because the long stems hang down, this plant needs to be elevated in some way. Bring it in before the first night frost and put it in a light, cool place (5-10°C, 41-50°F). Water very sparingly but take care that the root ball does not dry out.

Pests and diseases: *Russelia* is essentially trouble-free.

Propagation: propagate *Russelia* by division or by cuttings. The cuttings will root at a soil temperature of about 25°C (77°F).

Solanum

Origin: *Solanum* is a huge genus of more than 1500 species. Some of the species are suitable subjects for containers. *Solanum rantonnetti* is a shrub from South America. *S. crispum* and *S. jasminoides* are evergreen climbers from Brazil and Chile respectively. *Solanum* is a relative of the potato, as you can clearly see from the flowers. And as with the potato and many other members of the nightshade family, any fruits produced by *Solanum* are poisonous.

Description: *Solanum rantonnetti*

is a vigorous shrub with fairly large, long leaves. It blooms from early spring until late in the autumn. The violet-blue flowers have a yellow centre. With a degree of patience and some support you can create a standard from this plant. *S. crispum* is a climber, which can get up to 3 m (10 feet). The leaves are lance-shaped with slightly wavy edges. The lavender-blue flowers are carried in large clusters. The flowers of *S. jasminoides* are light blue and very like the flowers of the potato. This climber can grow as tall as 7 m (23 feet), but responds extremely well to pruning. Both *S. jasminoides* and the white-flowered cultivar 'Album' produce a profusion of flowers over a prolonged period. If the winter temperature is high enough, both these plants will to

continue to bloom even in the winter.

Care: *Solanum rantonnetti* is frost tender and consequently has to be brought in before the first night frost. *S. crispum* and *S. jasminoides* can stay out longer since they can withstand temperatures down to -5°C (23°F). All *Solanum* varieties like fertile soil in the form of ordinary potting compost with the addition of well-rotted farmyard manure. Repot young plants every year and older specimens every 2 or 3 years. Give them plenty of water during the growing season and feed them every other week with house plant fertilizer. They like a warm position in the summer and need a great deal of light. In the winter months they can be put in a cool place (about 5°C, 41°F), which may be dark. They will then lose their leaves and need much less water. You can cut them back hard before you put them in their winter quarters. When they begin to shoot again in spring, they need more light and water. Pinch out the side shoots several times to produce nice bushy plants.

Pests and diseases: in a warm overwintering place, some *Solanum* species can have problems with whitefly and aphids.

Propagation: propagate *Solanum* by rooting cuttings at a soil temperature of about 20°C (68°F).

Tecomaria

Origin: The climber *Tecomaria capensis* (Cape honeysuckle) hails from South Africa. Though it is not

Most container plants, like this Solanum, *need protection from bright sunlight for some time after they go back outside in the spring.*

a member of the honeysuckle family, the tubular flowers explain its common name. In its native habitat it can grow over 8 m (26 feet) high, but pruning will keep it much smaller. It will then become much more bushy and compact, so that it looks more like a shrub than a climber. Pruned in this fashion, it will not climb.

Description: the foliage of *Tecomaria capensis* is unevenly divided and the leaflets have slightly serrated edges. They are dark green and lustrous. The tubular flowers are carried in short spikes. These exotic-looking, showy flowers are

Musa coccinea.

Myrtus communis.

orange-red and do not appear until September and October.

Care: *Tecomaria* prefers a warm, sunny spot during the summer. If it is grown as a climber, it needs a support to climb up. Pruning the plant regularly will turn it into a bushy shrub. *Tecomaria* thrives in ordinary potting compost. Water copiously, but to promote flowering it is a good idea to skip a watering every now and then. It is frost tender, so it must be brought inside before the first night frost. Keep it in a cool, light place (5-10°C, 41-50°F) over the winter.

Pests and diseases: aphids may occasionally be a problem.

Propagation: you can raise *Tecomaria capensis* from seed, or you can root stem tip cuttings at a soil temperature of about 20°C (68°F).

Tibouchina

Origin: *Tibouchina urvilleana* (the glory bush) is a magnificent flowering plant from Brazil, where it grows into a shrub 5 m (16 feet) high. It also grows very vigorously in a pot, but pruning will keep it in check. It flowers in the winter months, producing large, velvety, purple-blue flowers.

Description: the leaves and stems of *Tibouchina* are closely covered with fine hairs, making them soft to the touch. The oval leaves are dark green. The flowers are a deep

purple-blue and seem to be made from velvet. They can grow as large as 10 cm (4 inches) across. The first flowers do not appear until August, but the plant will then go on flowering right through the autumn.

Care: *Tibouchina urvilleana* does not like full sun and does much better in a slightly shady spot on the patio. Because the stems are fairly slender and fragile, the plant also needs to be sheltered from the wind. Water freely during the summer, but make sure that the compost is well-drained. Grow *Tibouchina* in ordinary potting compost and repot every two or three years. Take care when repotting since the roots are delicate and easily damaged. Feed only occasionally. The first flowers will appear in August, and because the plant will flower until well into the winter it needs a light position and a temperature of about 10°C (50°F). Bring the plant in before the first night frost otherwise it will drop all its leaves and flowering will be poor. Water much more sparingly in winter.

Once the last flowers have faded in March, you should cut the plant back hard to encourage strong, bushy growth.

Continue pinching out the new shoots until mid-July, otherwise the stems will become straggly and break.

Pests and diseases: whitefly.

Propagation: root semi-ripe cuttings at a soil temperature of about 25°C (77°F).

Trachelospermum

Origin: *Trachelospermum jasminoides* is indigenous to East Asia. In hot climates it is used as an evergreen ground cover plant or as a climber. It grows slowly initially, but once it is established it can become very vigorous. *Trachelospermum* is a member of the same family as the oleander and all parts of the plant, like those of its relative, are poisonous.

Description: the leathery, glossy leaves of *Trachelospermum jasminoides* are dark green and oval. The white, highly fragrant flowers are about 2 cm (3/4 inch) across and are borne in clusters. Flowering can begin early in the spring and continue until well into the autumn. If it is given support it is a climber, otherwise it will trail or creep.

Care: *Trachelospermum* prefers a warm, sunny position, but will also flourish in light shade. It can go outside early and does not have to be brought back in again until quite late in the year since it is reasonably hardy (to -10°C, 14°F). In a mild winter, it can simply stay out. A cold spell probably encourages flowering, as does feeding in the spring and early summer. Plant *Trachelospermum* in general purpose potting compost and water regularly. Young plants should be repotted every year; older specimens need repotting only once every three years. There is no need to prune unless the plant gets too tall.

Viburnum tinus.

Jasminum officinale ‘*Grandiflorum*’.

Podranea ricasoliana.

Pests and diseases: *Trachelospermum* is prone to attack by mealy bug and scale insects.
In dark, wet places it will sometimes suffer from iron deficiency.
Propagation: you can propagate *Trachelospermum jasminoides* by taking stem cuttings. To do this, cut a stem into several pieces, all of which should root at a soil temperature of 25 to 30°C (77-86°F).

Viburnum

Origin: *Viburnum tinus* is a native of the Mediterranean region.
This evergreen shrub can grow to more then 5 m (16 feet) high in the wild. It is reasonably hardy and will survive outside during the winter in warmer parts of the country. Elsewhere it is wise to grow *Viburnum tinus* in a container, so that it can be brought inside if there is a very severe frost to overwinter safely.

Description: *Viburnum tinus* is an evergreen, bushy shrub with oval leaves which are light green on the underside and dark green and glossy on the top.
The plant comes into flower in the autumn and continues until late spring. The highly fragrant flowers are carried in flat heads. They are pink in the bud, turning gradually to white as they open. The flowers are followed by attractive dark blue berries.

Care: *Viburnum tinus* is an easy container plant. It thrives in ordinary potting compost with a little bit of clay or loam. Make sure the container is free-draining. Repot the plant once every three years and add organic fertilizer at that time.
It needs a lot of water during the summer - the root ball must never be allowed to dry out.
There is no need to bring the plant inside unless there is a very severe frost. It then needs a light, very cool place (0-5°C, 32-41°F). Cut right back on watering, but take care that the root ball does not dry out.

Pests and diseases: *Viburnum tinus* is essentially untroubled by pests and diseases.

Propagation: propagate *Viburnum tinus* by stem tip cuttings.

Zantedeschia

Origin: *Zantedeschia aethiopica* (arum lily) originates in marshy

areas of South Africa. It was named after an Italian botanist, Giovanni Zantedeschi, who described the plant and brought it to Europe in the eighteenth century. Nowadays, the unusual blooms of this plant are often sold as cut flowers.

Description: *Zantedeschia aethiopica* has arrow-shaped leaves. It blooms in spring and early summer. The funnel-shaped spathes are carried on stems 90 cm (3 feet) long. The yellow spadix is encircled by a white, partially recurved spathe. Below ground, *Zantedeschia* has thick, fleshy tubers.

Care: *Zantedeschia aethiopica* is a native of marshland, so it needs a great deal of water. It will even grow as a marginal plant in shallow water.

It is not hardy, however, so it is not a good idea to grow it in the garden pond. If you would like to grow it in water, it would be better to select a tub or pot that you can turn into a miniature pond. If you grow the plant in an ordinary pot, it prefers a potting compost with plenty of humus in it.

Repot every winter. Feed regularly with house plant food during the flowering period in the spring. *Zantedeschia* prefers a position in partial shade, protected from the heat of the midday sun.
Bring it inside before the first night frost and put it in a cool, light place (4-10°C, 39-50°F) for the winter.

Pests and diseases: *Zantedeschia* can be troubled by a harmless fungus which causes brown spots on the leaves. Remove the affected

Plumbago auriculata.

leaves. Fierce sun can also cause brown patches on the leaves.

Propagation: *Zantedeschia aethiopica* can be propagated by division. Carefully divide the plant into smaller pieces when repotting.

127

Plants and their attributes

Some of the attributes of plants are so important that they can be the decisive factor when it comes to making your choice. To make things easier for you, in this chapter I have listed the plants according to their different attributes.

Container plants

Fragrant
Brunfelsia calycina
Buddleia asiatica
B. globosa
Callistemon citrinus
Camellia sinensis
Citrus
Datura
Eriobotrya japonica
Eucalyptus citriodora
Hedychium
Heliotropium
Jasminum
Lantana
Laurus
Magnolia grandiflora
Mandevilla suaveolens
Myrtus
Olea europea
Oxypetalum caeruleum
Pittosporum tenuifolium

P. tobira
P. undulatum
Podranea
Trachelospermum jasminoides
Viburnum tinus

Poisonous
Cestrum
Datura stramonium
D.s. var. inermis
Lantana
Nerium
Solanum
Trachelospermum

Deciduous
Agapanthus
Bougainvillea
Cassia corymbosa
Cestrum
Chamaerops
Datura
Erythrina

Wooden tubs with curved handles are easy for two people to move.

Fuchsia
Hedychium
Lantana
Pelargonium
Pistacia
Solanum

Half hardy and frost hardy
Callistemon
Camellia
Cassia corymbosa
Chamaerops
Clianthus
Convolvulus cneorum
C. mauritanicus
Dicksonia antarctica
Eriobotrya

Jasminum nudiflorum
Laurus nobilis
Nandina
Nerium
Phoenix canariensis
Phormium
Pistacia
Pittosporum tobira
Podocarpus
Punica
Solanum crispum
S. jasminoides
Trachelospermum
Viburnum tinus

Annuals for containers

Antirrhinum
Brachycome
Clarkia
Diascia
Dimorphotheca
Erigeron

Lathyrus
Lobelia
Nemesia
Nicotiana
Nierembergia
Omphalodes
Pelargonium
Petunia
Silene
Tropaeolum
Verbena
Viola

Perennials and shrubs for containers

Bergenia
Buxus
Campanula
Erica
Euonymus
Euphorbia
ferns

A large Chinese pot with simple planting (in this case Euonymus) *can be an eye-catching feature in any garden.*

Hebe
Hedera
Helleborus
herbs
Hosta
Hydrangea
Lavandula
Rhus
Santolina
Saxifraga
Sedum
Teucrium

Bulbs for containers

Begonia
Canna
Crinum

129

Pistia stratiotes *(water lettuce)*.

Crocus
Dahlia
Eucomis
Galtonia
Hippeastrum
Lilium
Muscari
Narcissus
Nerine
Oxalis
Sprekelia
Tulip

Menyanthes
Myosotis
Nymphaea 'Pygmaea'
Rorippa
Sagittaria

Tender
Eichhornia
Nelumbo
Pistia

Water plants for containers

Hardy
Butomus
Caltha
Hydrocharis
Hydrocotyle
Iris siberica
Lemna
Lotus uliginosis

Glossary

In every book on gardening and every description of a plant -often on the packaging- you will find the same terms being used. Here is an explanation of some of them.

Miniature pond with Hydrocharis (frogbit).

Annuals Plants which germinate, flower and set seed in one season.

Cultivar A contraction of 'cultivated variety'. A plant produced by crossing which differs in appearance from its parents. The name of a cultivar, written with a capital letter and between inverted commas, is always given after the species name.

Cuttings Vegetative method of propagating plants by taking a portion of a plant and putting it into soil. Each piece develops roots and grows into a new plant. There are numerous types of cuttings, the principal ones being softwood (or stem tip) cuttings, semi-ripe cuttings and hardwood cuttings.

Dioecious Male flowers only or female flowers only on one plant. A male and a female individual are needed in order to set seed.

Division Vegetative method of propagating plants by dividing the root system and shoots into smaller pieces. Each piece grows into a new plant.

Drainage Drainage in a pot: a layer of coarse grit or crocks placed over the drainage holes at the bottom of a pot so that excess water can drain away quickly.

131

Hardening off	Allowing young plants to acclimatize to the less hospitable, or in any event different conditions outside in order to increase their chances of survival.
Hardy	Describes plants that survive winter conditions, including frost, without protection.
Humus	Dark, spongy matter in the soil, the residue of decayed and rotted vegetation and other organic materials.
Perennials	Herbaceous plants which generally die back in the autumn and come up again the following spring.
Pinching out	Removing the growing tip of a stem or branch, to encourage buds (growth points) lower down the stem to form side shoots.
Pricking out	Planting out seedlings into a larger tray or pot.
Seedlings	Very young plants grown from seed.
Shrubs	Woody-stemmed plants branched at or near the base. Deciduous shrubs drop their leaves in winter, leaving bare branches; evergreen shrubs retain their leaves.

A miniature garden has been created in this trough with a few perennials and some large rocks. The straight lines of the trough are reflected in the formal design of the garden.

Facing page: Hebe is an attractive shrub that does very well in a container. Some varieties are not fully hardy and will have to be brought indoors if there is a severe frost.

The rounded lines of the pot harmonize with the curving stems of the trailing begonia.

The flowers and leaves of most Oxalis species close at night and open again next day in the first rays of the sun.

Lenten rose 12

lily 13

lobelia 10

loquat 87

Lotus 102

L. berthelotii 102

L. maculatus 94, 102

L. muscaensis 102

Magnolia 103

M. grandiflora 103, 115

M.g. 'Maryland' 103

M.g. 'Russet' 103

Mandevilla 104

M. 'Alice du Pont' 104

M. 'Aphrodite' 96, 104

M. splendens 104

M. suaveolens 96, 104

marguerite 63, 80

Menyanthes 16

miniature date palm 114

Musa 104, 124

M. acuminata 'Dwarf Cavendish' 105

M. coccinea 105

M. x *paradisiacea* 105

myrtle 19, 105

Myrtus 39, 47, 105, 124

M. communis 106

M.c. var. *tarentina* 106

Nandina 106

N. domestica 106

N.d. 'Alba' 107

N.d. 'Compacta' 107

N.d. 'Nana' 107

N.d. 'Pygmaea' 107

nasturtium 11

Nelumbo 16

Passiflora caerulea.

Nemesia 11

Nerine 9, 13, 19, 20

Nerium 8, 107

N. oleander 45, 101, 107

New Zealand flax 10, 114

Nicotiana 11

Nierembergia 11

Nymphaea 'Pygmaea' 16

Olea 38, 39, 48, 109

O. europea 109

oleander 8, 9, 19, 107

olive 9, 38, 109

Omphalodes 11

Origanum rotundifolia 14

ornamental tobacco 11

Oxalis 13, 138

Oxypetalum 109

O. caeruleum 99, 109, 110

pansy 1, 10, 58

parrot's bill 84

passion flower 110

passion fruit 9

Passiflora 110

P. alata x *caerulea* 'Keizerin Eugenie' 112

P. caerulea 99, 110, 112, 139

P.c. 'Constance Elliott' 112

P. quadrangularis 112

P. violacea 98, 112

Pelargonium 9, 10, 12, 20, 41, 44, 53, 59, 61, 63, 100, 103, 110, 112, 117

P. peltatum 112

P. zonale 112

Pentas 12

petunia 10, 12, 41, 51

Phoenix 113

P. canariensis 113, 114

P. dactylifera 114

P. roebelenii 114

Phormium 10, 114

P. 'Atropurpureum' 115

Erythrina crista-galli.

Heliotropium arborescens.

P. 'Aureum' 115

P. 'Rubrum' 115

P. 'Variegatum' 115

P. colensoi 114, 115

P. tenax 114, 115

pistachio nut 115

Pistacia 115

P. lentiscus 115

P. terebinthus 115

P. vera 115

Pistia 16, 130

Pittosporum 70, 116

P. crassifolium 116

P. tenuifolium 116

P. tobira 70, 113, 116, 118

P. undulatum 116

plantain lily 12

Plumbago 117

P. auriculata 117, 118, 127

P.a. 'Alba' 117

Podocarpus 118

P. macrophyllus 118

Podranea 118, 126

P. ricasoliana 118, 120

pomegranate 120

Poncirus 82

Punica 120

P. granatum 120, 122

P.g. 'Nana' 120, 121

pygmy date palm 114

Rhodochiton 11, 12

rock rose 81

rosemary 9

Russelia 121

R. equisetiformis 102, 121

sacred lotus 16

Sagittaria 16

Scaevola 12, 54

Sedum 13

Silene 11

silky oak 94

Solanum 122, 123

S. crispum 122, 141

S. jasminoides 122

S.j. 'Album' 122

S. rantonnetti 110, 122

Sprekelia 6, 13

sweet bay 9, 19, 25, 37, 100

sweet pea 11

sweet pepper 9

Taxus 63, 118

Tecomaria 123

T. capensis 122, 123, 124

Tibouchina 105, 124

T. urvilleana 124

Trachelospermum 109, 125

T. jasminoides 114, 125, 126

Tropaeolum 11

T. majus 11

T. peregrinum 11

Tweedia caerulea,

    see *Oxypetalum caeruleum*

Verbena 11, 32

Viburnum 126

V. tinus 106, 125, 126

water hyacinth 16, 54

water lettuce 16, 130

Solanum crispum.

yew 63, 118

Zantedeschia 127

Z. aethiopica 100, 106, 127

Photograph credits

p. 143: the Abutilon's long flowering season makes it an extremely useful ornamental plant.

M. Hop: pp. 6 right, 7 (Mien Ruys' garden), 11 above, 14, 17 left, 19, 20, 24 left, 25, 26, 28 left, 30, 32, 34, 41 above, 42 (Mien Ruys' garden), 43, 44, 49, 54 below, 63, 65, 69, 70, 71, 76 left, 91 right, 92, 99 left, 102 right, 108 left, 115, 129, 132

G. M. Otter: pp. 8, 9, 13, 16, 18, 22, 23, 28 right, 29, 31, 35 above, 38, 39, 40, 45, 46 left, 47, 48, 50, 52, 53, 54 above, 57, 62, 64, 66, 67, 68, 72, 73 left, 74, 75 left, 76 right, 77, 78, 79, 80 left, 81, 82, 84 left, 85, 86, 87, 88 left, 90 left, 91 left, 93, 94, 95 right, 96 right, 97, 100, 102 left, 104 right, 105, 106 left, 107, 110 left, 112, 113, 114, 117, 120, 121 right, 122, 123, 124, 125, 126, 127, 130, 134, 137, 138, 139, 140 left, 141, 143

P. Schut: pp. 27, 33, 37, 55, 84 right, 128, 131

N. Vermeulen: back cover (below), title page, pp. 6 left, 10, 11 right, 12, 21, 24 right, 35 below, 36, 41 below, 46 right, 51, 56, 58, 59, 60, 61, 73 right, 75 right, 83, 88 right, 89, 90 right, 95 left, 96 left, 98, 99 right, 103, 104 left, 106 right, 108 right, 109, 110 right, 111, 116 left, 118, 119, 121 left, 133, 140 right

Acknowledgements
The publisher, author and photographers would like to thank
the following people and organizations for the willing assistance
they gave in the production of this book:
Priona gardens, Schuinesloot; Castle Gardens, Arcen;
De Egelantier, Paterswolde; De Kleine Plantage, Eenrum;
Huis De Dohm, Heerlen; Mien Ruys Model Gardens,
Dedemsvaart; De Rhulenhof, Ottersum; Castle Gardens, Wijlre;
Jan Boomkamp Model Gardens, Borne; Pastel Garden,
Sebaldeburen; Bert Nuis, Groningen; A. de Boer, Assen;
Ada Hofman Water Gardens, Loozen; Overhagen, Velp;
De Oranjerie, 's-Gravenzande; Oranjevereniging, Purmerend;
Trial Gardens, Delft; Mrs van Bennekom, Domburg;
Mrs Dekkers, Veere; the Poley family, Nisse.